WALKING IN DOMINION

D1253686

WALKING IN DOMINION

TOYE ADEMOLA

All Scripture quotations unless otherwise marked are taken from The New King James Version of the Holy Bible. Copyright © 1979, 1980, 1982, Thomas Nelson, Inc., Publishers.

Scripture quotations marked (KJV) are from the King James Version of the Holy Bible.

Take note that the name satan, related names, and references are not capitalized. We choose not to give him any respect, even to the point of violating grammatical rules.

Printed in Canada

Publishing services by Selah Publishing Group, LLC, Arizona. The views expressed or implied in this work do not necessarily reflect those of Selah Publishing Group.

ISBN 978-1-58930-168-9
Library of Congress Control Number: 2006900922

Dedicated to the Holy Spirit,
My Indispensable Friend

CONTENTS

WHY I WROTE THIS BOOK

There is an evil I have seen under the sun, as
an error proceeding from the ruler: Folly is set
in great dignity, while the rich sit in a lowly
place. I have seen servants on horses, while
princes walk on the ground like servants.

ECCLESIASTES 10:5–7

Nothing brings greater pain to my heart than to see
a Christian harassed and ruffled by the troubles of this
world. I hate to see a believer barely "surviving" in life,
"struggling" frantically with sin, disease, poverty, and
distress. It is so heart-wrenching to me.

Why should the rich sons of the Most **High** God sit
in **low** places? Why should the princes of the King of the
whole universe walk as mere servants in the earth? This
is an evil irony. It is a great error!

Unfortunately, this is the baffling experience of many
precious saints today. Very few are living in power and
victory. Many believers claim that they are the sons and

daughters of the King of kings, yet they are not living like princes. Instead, they are languishing as slaves in the earth.

They confess that they are redeemed and free, but they live as if they were still in bondage to the enemy. They are constantly under attack by the evils of sin, infirmities, addictions, and every form of satanic oppression.

Walking in Dominion is set on a revolutionary mission to correct these errors, which seem to be so widespread in the body of Christ today. My divine mandate in life is to help the people of God live in victory and power just as He has meant for us to live.

> *Walking in Dominion* is set on a revolutionary mission to correct these errors, which seem to be so widespread in the body of Christ today.

You see, I, too, like many believers today, used to live in despair and defeat. I have known firsthand what it means to struggle, suffer, barely making it in life. I can assure you, it is not a great way to live!

Though I became a born-again Christian in 1981, it was not until a few years after my conversion that I really began to enjoy what I call "the full benefits" of redemption.

Although I was a genuine believer, bought and washed by the blood of the Lamb ... though I was a true son of the King of kings ... in the earliest days of my

Christian experience, I did not live like a prince. Instead, I lived like a servant! I claimed to be free, yet in reality I did not live as if I were free. Sin and its awful consequences still seemed to have a stronghold on me.

At that period of my life, I was very vulnerable to sickness. I remember one particular time when I came down with a terrible disease. My illness was so serious that I had to be withdrawn from school and admitted into a hospital for quite a while. There I received several painful shots.

There was also the issue of poverty. Growing up as a child, all I ever knew was lack. I came from an extremely poor family. I lost my earthly father at the age of 11 months, and was raised by my grandmother. Her small earnings were scarcely enough to cover even our simplest needs. In those days, shoes, nice clothes, and toys were virtually out of my reach. As a matter of fact, I did not even own any shoes until I was a teenager! I lived in this state of abject poverty until young adulthood.

To my surprise, pain, stress, and suffering did not **automatically** disappear after I became born again. This perplexed me. If I had been redeemed from the curse of the law, why was I not experiencing the fullness of God's blessing? I knew something was definitely wrong because according to Deuteronomy 28:15–68, poverty and sickness, among other things, are curses. They are not blessings!

Suddenly, one day, it dawned on me—Jesus has <u>completely</u> redeemed me. He <u>finished</u> His work concerning my liberation. **He left nothing undone!** Therefore I did not have to live as a slave to sin. I did not have to struggle with any kind of bondage because when ... *the Son (Jesus) made me free, He made me free indeed* (John 8:34–35).

And "free" means **free**. A person who is really free does not live under the mastery or control of sin, addiction, sickness, or any form of satanic oppression. You cannot truly say that you are free if you still commit sin habitually. Jesus said, *"Most assuredly, I say to you, whoever commits sin is a slave of sin"* (John 8:34).

Beyond any shadow of doubt, I knew that because Jesus had made me free indeed, I did not have to live as a slave of sin. Instead, I could live as a son of God. As His son, the shackles of sin and every evil of life have completely lost their power over me. Therefore blessings, not curses, are my portion. Consequently, I made up my mind that sickness, poverty, and any form of curse would no longer be tolerated in my life.

DOMINION: THE MISSING LINK

> Then God blessed them, and God said to them, "Be fruitful and multiply; fill the earth and subdue it; **have dominion** over the fish of the sea, over the birds of the air, and over every living thing that moves on the earth."

> GENESIS 1:28

In Eden, Adam and Eve enjoyed a blessed and prosperous life **when they had dominion**. However, after they lost their dominion and authority, they began to experience a hard and laborious life.

It is no different with us today. Without dominion authority invested in us by God, it is impossible for us to experience a blessed life. This is the reason why when the Father made you and I His sons, He also gave us dominion and authority (John 1:12). Not only did He redeem us, He also gave us the right to rule in the earth. He empowered us so that we could have victory in all things and at all times.

On the basis of this, I began to understand that as believers, we do not need to experience defeat in life, not even for once! God wants us to always "triumph in Christ" (2 Corinthians 2:14). Yet **to experience a life of fulfillment and power, to enjoy the full blessings of redemption, a believer must know how to walk in dominion.** This is where I had missed it.

It dawned on me that the reason why I had experienced so much defeat and pain was because I had not learned how to exercise my God-given authority. Simply put, **I did not know how to walk in dominion**.

> It dawned on me that the reason why I had experienced so much defeat and pain was because I had not learned how to exercise my God-given authority. Simply put, I did not know how to walk in dominion.

However, as soon as I began to understand how to walk in my dominion authority, my life took a revolutionary turn. Fear, sickness, and poverty became things of the past. My financial situation radically changed. As a matter of fact, at one point the

Lord clearly spoke to me and said, *"Son, your days of suffering and shame are over. It is impossible for you to ever be poor again."*

The truth is, I have never quite been the same again. I quickly graduated from the low life, which I had known for so long, and I began to experience life on a higher dimension. I began to live what I call "the dominion lifestyle."Many Christians today are struggling like I did back then. This is because they have not yet understood how to walk in the dominion power and authority that is theirs in Christ. It is one thing for a person to be a **born-again** believer; it is another for him to know how to walk in dominion.

Most Christians know that heaven awaits them when they die, but they do not know how to live a life of power and authority here on the earth. One man of God put it this way, "Many believers know how to die, but they do not know how to live!"

Please understand that in Christ, you can have the best of both worlds—**abundant life on earth and eternal life in heaven!** God is not just concerned with your eternal destiny. He also wants you to have a life of victory and power here on earth right now! Your Savior and Lord has paid the price of your redemption IN FULL!

JESUS PAID FOR <u>ALL</u>. DO NOT SETTLE FOR <u>LESS</u>!

Let's suppose you go to your favorite retail shop to buy seven suits. After you have made your selection, you give the cashier the **complete** payment for your clothes. You then remember that you had to visit some other shops in the mall. So you politely ask the cashier

> In Christ, you can have the best of both worlds— **abundant life on earth and eternal life in heaven!**

to keep your clothes at his counter, promising that you would be back to pick them up on your way out. A few hours later, you return for your items. However to your surprise, without acknowledging your receipt, which proves that you have already made the full payment, the cashier gives you six suits instead of seven. Now what would you do at this point? Would you walk away and calmly say to yourself, *Well, six out of seven is not bad. I really do not care if I do not get my remaining suit?* No way! You would protest strongly. You would refuse to leave until he gave you your full purchase.

In the same way, Jesus paid the price for your salvation IN FULL. Do not accept anything less than what Jesus paid for! Do not settle for anything less than the FULL benefits of your redemption. Do not accept poverty. Jesus became poor so that you could be rich. Do not endure curses. Jesus became a curse so that you could enjoy all the blessings of God. Do not accept sickness or pain because by the stripes of Jesus you were healed.

> The **"Dominion Way"** is the God-ordained way to live!

Quite frankly, it is abnormal for a Christian to live his life any other way apart from the "dominion way." It is an abomination for any son or daughter of the Almighty, all-powerful God to be subdued by any kind of evil or oppression. It is totally unbecoming of your princely status. Friend, the "dominion way" is the God-ordained way for you to live.

When you know how to walk in dominion, you will live a life of power and fulfillment. You will not be dominated by curses. Instead, the blessings of the Lord will follow you and even overtake you. Deuteronomy 28:2

> Jesus paid the price for your salvation IN FULL. Do not accept anything less than what Jesus paid for!

Has your life been one constant struggle? Are you collapsing under the crushing weight of curses? Or do you simply desire to experience a life of ever-increasing blessedness, excellence, and intimacy with God? Then this book is a must-read for you.

Walking in Dominion will teach you how to consistently live in absolute victory. No longer will you be oppressed, suppressed, and depressed by the enemy! You will not be tossed and trampled by the woes of this world. Instead, you will discover how you can without fail keep satan under your feet!

Beloved, you do not have to put up with pain, defeat, and shame. You do not have to struggle with troubles and illness all your life. No. Total dominion is your portion in the Lord Jesus Christ!

So prepare to occupy the position of power and authority that is rightfully yours in Christ Jesus. Get ready to rise above every adversity and trouble of this world. You are a son or daughter of the King

> *Walking in Dominion* will teach you how to **consistently** live in **absolute** victory.

of kings. You were born to overcome all of life's woes. You were born to reign. You have been ordained to walk in dominion!

PART ONE

YOU ARE DESTINED FOR DOMINION

And God said, Let us make man in our image,
after our likeness: and **let them have dominion**...

GENESIS 1:26

CHAPTER ONE
WHAT IS DOMINION?

Before I define what *dominion* is, it is important that I first clarify what dominion is not.

Dominion **IS NOT** the oppressive domination of fellow human beings. The forceful subjugation of people is totally contrary to God's greatest commandment, which is to love. No person has the right to manipulate or intimidate another. Such control is sheer wickedness. It is witchcraft!

So what **IS** dominion? The word *dominion* is the Hebrew word RADAH (pronounced *raw-daw*). *Radah* means to have authority, to reign, to govern, and to be in charge. It also means to subdue, subjugate, to prevail against, to trample on, and to tread down. Lastly, it means to master and to lead.

This definition reveals three key aspects of dominion. When God said '...*Let them have dominion...*,' He had all three dimensions in mind. He wants you to experience dominion on all three of these levels. He created you to have complete (not partial) dominion.

On the basis of this definition, dominion is: (1) your CROWN of glory, (2) your CONQUERING power, and (3) your divine CAPABILITY.

DOMINION IS YOUR CROWN OF GLORY
"Let them… reign, rule, govern, be in charge."

> What is man that You are mindful of him, and the son of man that You visit him? For You have made him a little lower than the angels, and **You have crowned him with glory and honor. You have made him to have dominion** over the works of Your hands; You have put **all things** under his feet.
>
> *PSALM 8:4–6*

When you think of the word *crown*, what comes to your mind? Most likely it is the image of a royal monarch upon whose head proudly rests a golden crown. Well, through dominion, God has also placed upon your head a crown of glory and honor. As a believer in Christ Jesus, God has crowned you a king.

> To Him who loved us and washed us from our sins in His own blood, and has made us kings and priests to His God and Father, to Him be glory and dominion forever and ever. Amen.
>
> *REVELATION 1:5B–6*

Jesus loved us. He washed us in His blood. But He did not stop there. He redeemed us to God … and made us kings … and we shall reign on the earth!

"You are worthy to take the scroll, and to open its seals; For You were slain, and have redeemed us to God by Your blood out of every tribe and tongue and people and nation, **and have made us kings and priests to our God; and we shall reign on the earth.**"

REVELATION 5:10B–11

Just as the kings and sovereigns of this world rule and have absolute control over their domains, God has made the earth your jurisdiction. Literally, the whole world is your domain. Everywhere you go in this world—wherever the soles of your feet trod—you have the divine authority to reign and dominate in it.

Your prosperity and promotion in life does not depend upon the country in which you live. Wherever you live— whether it is a *first-* or *third*-world country, a poor or rich nation, a developed or developing country—you are destined to reign and prosper there. Your redemption qualifies you to reign as king in the whole earth.

It does not even matter whether or not you are a citizen of the land in which you live—your dominion qualifies you to be favored and blessed in every nation on earth! God has crowned you with glory and honor, and empowered you to have dominion wherever the soles of your feet shall tread.

This was the mentality I had when I relocated from my native country, Nigeria, to the United States over a decade ago. I never for one moment considered that I was just an immigrant. No! I did not come to the

United States as a foreigner. I came as a God-appointed king with legal rights and access to all nations, including America. As far as I was concerned, America was **my** country.

At first, when I had just arrived, the enemy tried to fill my mind with fear saying, *This country is tough on foreigners. You will be discriminated against. Your accent will limit you. It is also a land that swallows up its inhabitants. There are bills to pay. No one will help you. You are on your own. Unless you struggle and work two (or even three) jobs, you cannot survive.* But glory to God, the Holy Ghost was quick to lift up His divine standard of truth against the devil's lies. He told me that God had not sent me here to struggle. God had sent me to the United States of America to reign!

With this fresh revelation of my kingship and authority, I chose to stay focused on the work of the ministry. I refused to walk by sight or be moved by the opinions of men. I refused to see the "giants" of America. I only focused on the greatness of my God!

> Your prosperity and promotion in life does not depend upon the country in which you live....Your dominion qualifies you to be favored and blessed in every nation on earth!

I am glad to say, my obedience and faith have greatly paid off. God has given me amazing success by His power. I have never once had to struggle or put myself under any kind of undue pressure. I have never depended on man for assistance. I have only relied on the One who crowned me king and gave me the dominion authority to rule in the country where He had sent me. I can truly say that God has showed me great favor in America. Her bounties flow ceaselessly in my direction. God loads me *daily* with benefits. He continues to bless and enlarge me in every aspect. To Him be all the glory!

If you ever find yourself living in a land that is not your native country, do not for once consider yourself to be **just an immigrant**. You are a king! Have the mentality of a king. Refuse to see the land that you are living in as a foreign land. When you view it as your country, it will favor you.

Remember Daniel, Joseph, Esther, and Mordecai? Not only did these great biblical heroes prosper in foreign lands, they also rose to positions of prominence and honor. Do not let the giants of race, accent, and so forth limit or intimidate you. You have authority in all the earth. The country where you now live is your domain. The milk and the honey of the land must flow to you. All you need is a revelation that you are a king. Whether or not you are a citizen of the country in which you live, your dominion authorizes you to prosper there!

THE POWER AND PRIVILEGES OF A KING

Through dominion, you have certain kingly powers and privileges. God has crowned you with glory and honor. The word *crown* means "to surround." As a God-appointed king in the earth, you are literally *enveloped* with all the splendor and dignity that is associated with divine royalty.

After his coronation, a king ceases to be an ordinary man. He does not live an average lifestyle, either. His crown is a symbol of the power, wealth, and dignity that befits his great status.

But you are a chosen generation, a royal priest-
hood, a holy nation, His own special people, that
you may proclaim the praises of Him who called
you out of darkness into His marvelous light.

1 PETER 2:9

In Christ you are royalty. You are a star. Never view yourself as an ordinary human being. No! You are exceptional.
You are a first-class citizen. You are a highly privileged individual. You are not a **COMMONER**. You are a
COMMANDER of wonders!

You are also a controller of vast wealth. As a God-
appointed king in the earth, you need to understand
that all the earth's immeasurable possessions are available to you. After God created the whole earth, He
gave man the title deed to the world. The earth is
man's domain. It is his to govern, manage, and control.

The heavens are the Lord's heavens, but the
earth has He given to the children of men.

PSALM 115:16 (AMP)

God has given you **all** things richly to enjoy. It is not
God's will for you to live in penury and want. A king does
not live in lack and want because he has all the resources of
his kingdom at his disposal. Think about it, have you ever
heard of a poor king in a wealthy domain?

With your dominion authority and power, there is no limit to what you can attain or have in life. The whole earth, in all its richness and fullness, belongs to you. God has given you all things that pertain to life and godliness. There is literally nothing that is impossible for you.

Nothing in this world—a failing economy, dysfunctional family background, or hostile social environment—has the power to limit you. You are above them all. They are your subjects; you are their king. Go forth in your dominion power and authority and possess your possessions, in Jesus' name!

> In Christ you are ROYALTY! ...You are not a COMMONER! You are a COMMANDER of wonders!

A KING'S ASSIGNMENT

It is important to mention at this point that the power and privileges of a king also come with great responsibility. God has not made you a king in the earth for your own selfish gain. Rather, He has placed you in a position of prominence for His own purpose. Though you are a king, you are still God's subject. He is the King of all kings!

As His king, you must submit yourself totally to Him. You must abide by His laws. You must not live your life as if it were your own. On the contrary, you must live for God and God alone.

Use whatever talent, wealth, position, and gifts He has given you for His purposes alone. Please understand that every blessing that God has given you is for a specific God-ordained purpose.

For example, He gives you children for signs and wonders (Isaiah 8:18). He has given you the power to get wealth so that He can establish His covenant (Deuteronomy 8:18). He has blessed you to be a blessing. So whatever God gives you must be used to glorify Him and serve His kingdom purpose.

God is like the Chief Executive Officer of a large multinational corporation who delegates authority to several regional directors in various countries. He gives them the legal right and power to act on his behalf. He also equips them with every resource that they would need. Having thus empowered his directors, the CEO trusts them to wisely use the resources that he has given them to promote the interest of the company. The directors must assume full responsibility of their respective locations. It would be irresponsible for them to expect the CEO to perform their duties.

Through dominion, the God of the whole universe has made you a *director* in the earth. He has given you the "power of attorney" to promote His kingdom. He has appointed you to act on His behalf on earth, as a "god" to the sons of men.

> I said, "You are gods, and all of you are children of the Most High."

> PSALM 82:6

When God was sending Moses to Pharaoh, He said to him, *"...I have made you as god to Pharaoh..."* (Exodus 7:1). Moses, in this capacity, was God's representative to Pharaoh. Each time Moses addressed Pharaoh, he did so with all the authority and power of God. In like manner, God has given you the power to enforce His authority in the world. He has placed all of the earth's resources under your control so that you can execute His purposes.

> So God created man in His own image, in the image and likeness of God He created him; male and female He created them. And God blessed them and said to them, **Be fruitful, multiply, and fill the earth, and subdue it [using all its vast resources in the service of God and man]**; and have dominion over the fish of the sea, the birds of the air, and over every living creature that moves upon the earth.
>
> GENESIS 1:27–28 (AMP)

Can God count on you to use your God-given assets to accomplish His purposes? Are you using your resources to serve God and humanity? Or are you selfishly keeping them to yourself? God has given you money. Do you control it, or does it control you? Are you faithful with your gifts? Never forget that you are God's steward in the earth. Your primary responsibility in life is to be faithful with everything that God gives you. Use your gifts—your power, position, and possessions for His glory alone.

A KING'S WORD IS POWER

Whenever a king makes a proclamation or decree, it is binding on his subjects. His word is law. His word is power. Nobody dares challenge or come against the word of the king.

> Where the word of a king is, there is power; and who may say to him, "What are you doing?"

ECCLESIASTES 8:4

God has given you great power to decree and establish by the word of your mouth. This is why you cannot afford to speak carelessly. Because you are a king, your word—good or bad—will surely come to pass.

> Adam exercised his dominion authority by the power of his word. Whenever Adam wanted something done, he **declared** and **decreed** it into being.

Divination is on the lips of the king; His mouth must not transgress in judgment.

PROVERBS 16:10

In Eden, Adam was king. He had the legal authority to take charge of everything that God had created. He was in absolute control of his world!

Then the LORD God took the man and put him in the Garden of Eden **to tend** and **keep it**.

GENESIS 2:15

Adam exercised his dominion authority by the power of his word. Whenever Adam wanted something done, he **declared** and **decreed** it into being. After God had created all the animals, He left their naming entirely up to Adam. Whatever name he called them became permanent.

> Out of the ground the LORD God formed every beast of the field and every bird of the air, and brought them to Adam to see what he would call them. And whatever Adam called each living creature, that was its name.
>
> GENESIS 2:19

Could God not have named the animals Himself? Of course He could. But He chose not to. He chose rather to bring them to Adam. Why? He brought the animals to Adam because he was the king of Eden. The earth was his jurisdiction. It was Adam's, not God's, responsibility to oversee its affairs. So, right from the very dawn of human history, God established an ageless principle: The **earth is man's domain. God would do nothing on the earth without the agreement and participation of man.** God will never circumvent the human will!

Beloved, in your mouth lays the power to take charge of anything that comes your way. You can literally chart the course of your situation, for better or for worse, by the power of your tongue. You **will** have what you say!

> Death and life are in the power of the tongue, and those who love it will eat its fruit.
>
> PROVERBS 18:21

This is why God's Word strongly admonishes you—**Do not say what you do not want!** Isaiah 33:24 says, *"And the inhabitant will not say, 'I am sick'…"* If you do not want sickness, do not say that you are sick. If you do, you will be sick. If you do not want poverty, do not say that you are poor. If you do, you will be poor. You will have what you say!

In contrast, when you decree what you desire, you will have what you want. When you speak in your kingship authority, your situations and circumstances will listen. Things will change for the best.

Do not be intimidated by the raging winds of life. You are a king. The control is in your hands. Take charge. Turn things around by the words of your mouth. If you feel weak, decree that you are strong. If you feel poor, decree that you are rich. As you decree, so shall it be!

> Thou shalt also decree a thing, and it shall be established unto thee: and the light shall shine upon thy ways.
>
> Job 22:28

When faced with a storm of life, Jesus did not fret. NO! He knew that He was a King. He knew that as a King, He was not subject to the negativities of the earth. Rather, the earth, including its weather, was subject to Him. So He took authority over the storm and commanded the fierce winds to cease (Matthew 8:23–27).

Then He arose and rebuked the winds and the sea, and there was a great calm.

MATTHEW 8:26

Beloved, I know that we live in a troubled and dangerous world. Storms of life are bound to come. But though you cannot stop the contrary winds of life from blowing in your direction, by your dominion authority you have the power to bring every storm under control. You can change the course of events from bad to good. You can turn the tide.

Jesus Himself testified that in the world we would have tribulation. But I am so glad that He did not stop there. He also said, "Be of good cheer, I have overcome the world."

"These things I have spoken to you, that in Me you may have peace. In the world you will have **tribulation**; but be of good cheer, I have overcome the world."

JOHN 16:33

In Christ there is peace. In the world there is tribulation. Now I ask you—are you in the world or are you in Christ? If you know and believe that you are in Christ ... if you know that you are born of God ... you can rest assured that you can overcome the troubles of the world (1 John 5:4).

> Though you cannot stop the contrary winds of life from blowing in your direction, by your dominion authority you have the power to bring every storm under control.

Are you facing a storm today? Understand that peace, not tribulation, is your portion. His power in you is far greater than all the troubles of the world put together. Nothing on earth has the power to overcome you. You are a king! You have been given the power to rule and reign over all.

Like Jesus, you can rebuke the wind and establish the peace of God in your life. Put your dominion power to work. Take authority over every contrary wind of your life. Rebuke the storm by the power of God's Word in your mouth. You are a king, and you must reign in the earth.

CHAPTER TWO

DOMINION IS YOUR CONQUERING POWER

"Let them ... subdue, subjugate, prevail against, trample on, and tread down."

The world is like a fiery battle zone. The forces of darkness are constantly waging war against all that is of God. Many have often wondered, *Why do bad things happen?* Well, the answer is quite simple—because there is a bad devil on the rampage. He literally goes to and fro on the whole earth seeking for human prey to devour.

Ever since he was cast out of heaven, satan's full-time job has been to wreak havoc on all mankind. His mission has been to *weaken the nations*—to steal, kill, and destroy anything and anyone on the earth.

> How you are fallen from heaven, O Lucifer, son of the morning! How you are **cut down to the ground**, you who weakened the nations!
>
> ISAIAH 14:12

After God placed Adam in Eden, He commanded him to *keep it* (Genesis 2:15). The word *keep* literally means "to guard" or "to protect." Now, the need to guard or protect anything or anyone would only arise from the presence of real danger.

Without an enemy, there would be no threat of harassment. There would be no need to be vigilant or *beef up* security. I really believe that when God instructed Adam to "keep" the garden, He was essentially asking him to keep Eden safe from the plundering pranks of the devil, the arch-enemy of God, who was now on the loose having been evicted from heaven due to his revolt.

However, God not only commanded Adam to *keep* the garden, He also empowered him. He gave him dominion—the conquering power that he would need to *subdue, subjugate, prevail against, trample on, and tread down* the devil.

Sadly, both Adam and his wife, Eve, failed to use their dominion authority against the devil. As a result, instead of subjugating satan, they became subdued by him. They became his victims. Through his evil subtlety, satan caused Adam and Eve to lose the wonderful garden that God had given them. Ultimately the entire human race became subject to the devil's evil reign.

But to God be the glory, in Christ, your dominion authority is restored! You do not have to lose your *garden*. You can keep everything that God has given you because you are no longer under satan's evil domination.

Inasmuch then as the children have partaken of flesh and blood, He Himself likewise shared in the same, that through death He might destroy him who had the power of death, that is, the devil, and release those who through fear of death were all their lifetime subject to bondage.

HEBREWS 2:14–15

On the contrary, it is the devil that is under you. You are above him. God has given you dominion over him. He has given you the ability to conquer and dominate every force of hell that ever comes against you.

And He (Jesus) said unto them, I beheld satan as lightning fall from heaven. Behold, I give unto you power to tread on serpents and scorpions, and over all the power of the enemy: and nothing shall by any means hurt you.

LUKE 10:19–20

Did you notice the verse says that you have power over all *not some of* the power of the enemy? Your dominion puts you in a position of absolute authority over satan and all his cohorts. Just think about that! If you have all power over the enemy, it simply follows that he definitely has no power over you.

Just because you belong to God, the devil hates you with a hatred that is simply beyond imagination. Any friend of God is a sworn enemy of the devil. As a result, satan will literally do everything within his power to hurt or harm you. He will try to rob you of every good and perfect gift that God has given you. He will try his best to challenge and subvert every good plan of God for your life.

> If you have ALL POWER over the enemy, it simply follows that he definitely has NO POWER over you!

But when you know how to walk in the dominion authority and power that is yours through Christ, NO THING— no weapon, no enchantment, no terror, no wile, no evil from the pit of hell—has the power to hurt you. Nothing shall by any means hurt you. Absolutely NOTHING!

"...**No weapon** formed against you shall prosper, and every tongue which rises against you in judgment you shall condemn. This is the **heritage** of the servants of the Lord, and their righteousness is from Me," says the Lord.

ISAIAH 54:17

For there is no sorcery against Jacob, nor any divination against Israel. It now must be said of Jacob and of Israel, 'Oh, what God has done!'

NUMBERS 23:23

Dominion is your *heritage* in Christ! It is your birthright as a son of the Most High God. Because you belong to Him, you are guaranteed victory over every weapon and sorcery of the enemy. You have the power that you need to overcome all the evils and troubles of the world.

Though the world is a *war zone* with turbulence and crisis all around, you do not have to be a casualty of war. In Christ, you are not a victim. You are a victor! You are not prey for the devil's consumption. You are more than a conqueror. (See Romans 8:37.)

DOMINION IS BY RIGHT NOT MIGHT

Please understand that the word *power* in Luke 10 does not refer to human might. Ephesians 6:10–12 makes it clear that our war is against the spiritual forces of hell.

> Finally, my brethren, be strong in the Lord and in the power of His might. Put on the whole armor of God, that you may be able to stand against the wiles of the devil. For we do not wrestle against flesh and blood, but against principalities, against powers, against the rulers of the darkness of this age, against spiritual hosts of wickedness in the heavenly places.

It is impossible to fight spiritual enemies with physical strength. Your strength against the enemy lies in the power of God's might, not human ability. As many as believe in the Lord Jesus Christ, He gives the right, the dominion authority, to reign as sons of God in the earth. Your divine authority as a believer connects you to the invincible power of God.

To better understand the power of authority as opposed to the power of human might, let us consider the analogy of a traffic policeman. A 150-pound policeman can stop a large, heavy-duty 18-wheeler truck dead in its tracks by merely raising up his hand, because of his authority. On the other hand, if he attempted to stop the truck with his physical might, he would be crushed in an instant. Why is this so? Well, he can control such a massive truck without even touching it simply because he has the authority of the United States government vested in him.

The truck driver stops because he knows that he is not just facing one policeman. He is actually facing an entire government! It is the same in the spiritual realm. When you come against the enemy in the authority of the Lord, satan knows that he is not just facing you. In reality, he is also facing the Almighty God.

When Jesus said, "I give you power…," He was in essence saying, *"I give you the divine authority and right to control everything that may come against you. Not by your physical might but through the invincible power of the Almighty God who backs you."*

You dare not stand against the devil in your own strength. You would be terribly outmatched. The devil is older than our oldest ancestor. You could say he's been there and done that. Nothing that human wisdom or might has to offer can move him. But when you stand against the enemy in your God-given dominion authority, the devil does not see you, he sees God in you. He sees the entire armies of heaven standing behind you ready to unleash God's power against him in full force and fury.

Quite often you will hear people say, "This circumstance is just beyond my control!" Beloved, you need to know that by virtue of your dominion authority, there is no circumstance that is out of your control.

No matter how large or intimidating a situation may seem, you have dominion authority over it. You can stop the enemy from advancing toward you the same way a policeman, exercising his authority, stops a huge truck in its tracks. That is how great the power of authority is!

In a very real sense, believers are spiritual policemen charged by God with the responsibility of enforcing His law and order in the earth. Like Jesus who came to destroy the works of the devil, we have been given power to subdue, defeat, and destroy every evil activity of hell.

The devil is the universe's worst criminal. He is a *thief, killer*, and *destroyer* by profession. But just as a policeman has the authority to capture criminals, God has given you authority to *arrest* the devil's activities in your life and the lives of others. You should never allow the enemy to have his way in your life. God has given you dominion. Arrest the devil. Subdue him under your feet.

The problem with many Christians today is that they are repeating the same mistake that Adam and Eve made in Eden. They are not using their dominion authority against the enemy. By being passive, they are in reality *allowing* the devil to have a *field day* in their lives. They let him have his way and *allow* him to bring bad things into

> Just as a policeman has the authority to capture criminals, God has given you authority to "arrest" and stop the devil's activities in your life and the lives of others.

their life. Sadly, some believers feel so helpless that they have resigned themselves to accept pain or bad occurrences as *necessary* evils of life.

EVIL IS NOT NECESSARY. IT IS OPTIONAL

Contrary to what some people believe, you do not have to experience evil. You can choose not to go through bad experiences. You can choose to live a tragedy-free life. As far as God is concerned, evil is not necessary; it is optional!

> See, I have set before you today life and good, death and evil. ... I have set before you life and death, blessing and cursing; therefore choose life, that both you and your descendants may live.
>
> *DEUTERONOMY 30:15,19*

Good or evil? It is obvious from this verse that the choice is yours. It is not up to God. It is up to you to make the decision whether to live in victory or be subdued in defeat. But God categorically instructs you to choose good and reject evil.

> Evil is not **necessary. It is optional. You do not have to accept negative things!**

Do not accept anything evil because God has destined only good for your life. There is no trace of evil or "badness" in the purpose of God for you!

For I know the thoughts that I think toward you,
says the LORD, thoughts of peace and not of evil,
to give you a future and a hope.

JEREMIAH 29:11

Beloved, please understand that evil is not necessary. It is optional! You do not have to accept negative and hurtful things. You can choose not to put up with anything that is not beneficial to you or your loved ones. Anything that is detrimental or damaging to your well-being is simply not of God. All of God's plans for you are good, and they are good all the time!

KINGDOM COMES BY FORCE

When you know how to walk in dominion, your life will literally be a *heaven-on-earth* experience. As a born-again believer, you are a citizen of heaven, and you are fully entitled to a heavenly lifestyle. Whatever does not exist in heaven must not be permitted in your life. Now you know that sin, poverty, fear, death, disease, and so forth cannot be found in heaven. Therefore, determine not to allow such things in your life also.

Yet, the kingdom lifestyle will not come to you by chance. The kingdom must be taken by force!

And from the days of John the Baptist until now
the kingdom of heaven suffers violence, and
the violent take it by force.

MATTHEW 11:12

Please understand that evil will not stay away from you or your loved ones simply because you **wish** against it. Evil will stay away because you **war** against it. If you are not ready to exercise and enforce your dominion authority over evil and death, you will not be able to choose good and life. In short, kingdom comes by power!

> Evil will not stay away from you or your loved ones simply because you **wish** against it. No! Evil will stay away because you **war** against it!

Beloved, the devil is all out on a ruthless mission to steal, kill, and destroy you (John 10:10). He has a **hell-bent** determination to ruin you. But any time it seems as if he is advancing toward your camp, anytime you feel as if every demon in hell has been set loose against you or your loved ones, do not despair. Do not be afraid. Meet the enemy **head-on** with force!

Use the dominion authority that God has given you to stop the devil in his tracks. Put an end to all his harassments. Your dominion power is a force that no demon in hell can withstand or stop.

It is only those who are willing to resist and fight the devil who will ever experience victory in life. There is no honor or glory for those who give up and surrender. On the other hand, whenever you resist the devil, he will flee.

> Submit yourselves therefore to God. Resist the
> devil, and **he will flee from you**.
>
> JAMES 4:7

Notice that in James 4:7, the Bible does not say to ignore the devil and hopefully after a while he will leave you
alone. No! It says to *resist* him. The devil, your chief adver-
sary, is not a gentleman. You must tackle him with force,
and not with diplomacy. Aggressively stop him from bring-
ing sickness, disease, defeat, failure, and every calamity of
life on you or your loved ones.

Today, many are not *rejecting* evil. They are not doing
anything to stop the oppressive activities of the devil in
their lives. A policeman's authority is useless if he cannot
use it to bring criminals to justice. In the same way, your
dominion authority will do you no good if you do not use
it to stop the enemy from plundering your life and the lives
of those around you. Any time the devil tries to bring evil
your way, do not be passive. Resist him! Refuse curses.
Choose the blessings of God. Do not endure evil and pain
any longer.

You need to understand one thing about the devil. If
you give him an inch, he will take a mile. If you do not
resist him when he brings sickness against you, the
next thing he will do is attack you in another area of
your life. If you let him have your marriage, he will go
for your career next. If you let him attack your finances, he will feel free to go after your health. You
simply cannot let the devil have any leeway in your
life. Anything that is permitted ultimately increases in

frequency. This is why you cannot condone or tolerate anything negative in your life. Evil left unconquered soon multiplies in catastrophic proportions!

There is an adage that says, "If you want to dine with the devil, you must use a long spoon." I prefer to say, "Do not dine with the devil at all!" Do not give him any leeway in your life. Anything that *smells* of the devil must not be allowed a moment's space in your life. Do not condone or tolerate anything negative in your life. Resist the enemy by force.

Remember, the devil has absolutely no authority over you. It is you who have absolute power over him. God has given you dominion, the conquering force that you need to crush him under your feet. Yes! You have what it takes to send the devil packing. You have the ability to stop him dead in his tracks. God has given you the conquering power to subdue, subjugate, prevail against, trample on, and tread down *"all the power of the enemy: and nothing shall by any means hurt you."*

CHAPTER THREE

DOMINION IS YOUR DIVINE CAPABILITY

"Let them... have the mastery; let them take the lead."

Mediocrity is foreign to God. All His works bear the mark of His excellence. In the creation of the world, God made sure that everything that He had created was not just good ... it was **very** good.

And God saw **every thing** that he had made, and, behold, it was very good. And the evening and the morning were the sixth day.

GENESIS 1:31

Through dominion, God also gave man the ability to excel at whatever it was that he did. Adam was by all standards a genius of the highest order. With his incredible mind he single-handedly named every animal on Planet Earth.

As a believer, you have a mind that is more extraordinary than any ordinary human being. You have the mind of Christ. You have the ability to imagine and innovate far above your unbelieving counterparts. Through Christ, and by the power of His mind at work in you, you can do all things.

> I can do all things through Christ who strengthens me.
>
> PHILIPPIANS 4:13

Today, unbelievers who do not possess the mind of Christ seem to be dominating various fields of human endeavor. This is an error that must be corrected. It is Christians who should be in the forefront of development. We have the mind of the One who created all things. We have the mind of Christ. It is time for believers to rule and dominate every arena of human enterprise for the glory of our God.

Beloved, God made you for **mastery**. Do not settle for **mediocrity**. It is so sad today that under the guise of *humility* many believers compromise on quality. In many Christian circles, excellence has been wrongly equated to worldliness. This is a lie from the pit of hell! If this has been your way of thinking, you need to change your mind now.

> Beloved, God made you for **mastery**. Do not settle for **mediocrity**!

Your God is a God of excellence. Just take a look at God's glorious creation ... the big blue sky, the star-studded galaxies, the cascading snow-capped mountains, the shimmering waterfalls, the brightly colored flowers, even the human body ... all of God's works are wonderfully and superbly made. He does not do shoddy jobs. Neither should you!

He has destined you for a life of success and distinction. He has crowned you with glory and honor so that you can dominate and excel in whatever you do. Consider all the patriarchs of old: Abraham, Isaac, Joseph, Job, Daniel ... all were men of great wealth, wisdom, and power. God wants you to be extremely successful in life. He has ordained you to be a person of influence, affluence, and excellence. You were created to be on top, not beneath!

> And the LORD will make you the head and not the tail; you shall be above only, and not be beneath, if you heed the commandments of the LORD your God, which I command you today, and are careful to observe them.
>
> DEUTERONOMY 28:13

In the secular world, outstanding athletes are said to *dominate* their fields. Tiger Woods, the most famous golfer in the world, is currently dominating the game of golf. In the kingdom of golf, Tiger is king! In Michael Jordan's day, he dominated the field of basketball. But as a born-again believer who possesses the mind of Christ, you are at a far greater advantage to excel than any secular celebrity in the world today.

Whatever you do, do not *just do it*. Do it excellently well! Always strive for the best. Do not do anything in a substandard way. God created you with an above-average capability to excel in whatever it is you lay your hands upon. As a believer, you have an above average IQ. You have the mind of Genius Himself. You have the mind of Christ. Do not settle for anything less than the best. Hate the words *mediocrity* and *average* with a passion. You are created to be a master in your career!

> For "who has known the mind of the Lord that he may instruct Him?" But we have the mind of Christ.
>
> 1 CORINTHIANS 2:16

Can you imagine a world where believers in Christ are the best at everything? A place where the best physicians, scientists, educators, inventors … were all Christians? How wonderful that would be! What great glory and honor that would bring to our God. Whenever believers excel in an extraordinary way, others stand at attention.

> Whatever you do, do not *just do it*. Do it excellently well!

Back in Daniel's day, God's wisdom in him commanded the respect and reverence of an ungodly king. As a result, King Nebuchadnezzar made a proclamation in all the land that the God of Daniel was the true God and He alone was to be worshipped (Daniel 2:46-49).

It can happen again in our day. Our excellence can testify, before unbelievers, of the greatness and goodness of our God. Our excellence can be a great evangelical tool, which reaps souls for Christ. So strive for excellence and distinction in all that you do. The unsaved will take notice and see God's glory in you. They will bow in surrender to His wisdom, salvation, and might, just as King Nebuchadnezzar did before Daniel. When we shine and excel in our endeavors, the world will see and glorify God in us *(Matthew 5:13-16)*.

DISCOVER YOUR DOMINION DOMAIN

Now, please understand that no human being can *dominate* every field of endeavor. That honor is reserved for Almighty God alone. Only He is omniscient and omnipotent. Many do not experience dominion in their undertakings because they lack focus. They keep trying their hands at too many things without actually mastering anything.

If you want to be the master or leader that God has ordained you to be, you need to identify what I call your unique *dominion domain*. It is the specific area of expertise in which God has ordained for you to shine in life. Though you may possess many skills,

> Your ability to recognize and diligently develop your most dominant skill is the first step to attaining excellence and success in life.

one skill will be more dominant than the others. There is something that you are uniquely good at. There is something for which God has specifically anointed you to excel in.

Years ago, one of my spiritual sons experienced a radical financial turnaround after he discovered his dominion domain. At the time, he was a college student who worked part-time at a local grocery store to sustain himself. The pay was low, and his hours were minimal. By the end of each month, he could barely keep up with his bills. Then one day, inspired by one of my messages, he decided to seek the Lord for direction and help in locating his unique skill.

The Lord quickened his heart to remember that he was exceptionally good at math. It then occurred to him that he could start his own tutoring business. God opened incredible doors for him. In a very short while, he had a substantial pool of students. He was so successful at tutoring that in his first year he made much more than he had ever earned working in his old job. His life has never been the same since then. Today he continues to excel as a successful Information Technology professional.

When Moses was about to begin construction of the tabernacle, he did not assign tasks indiscriminately. Following God's specific instructions, he gave the workers jobs comparable to their unique skills. He recognized the fact that no one is good at everything. God has specially given each person divine capabilities for specific tasks. Good examples of this were Bezalel and Aholiab, two of Israel's most skilled artisans:

And Bezalel and Aholiab, and every gifted arti-
san in whom the LORD has put wisdom and
understanding, to know how to do all manner
of work for the service of the sanctuary, shall do
according to all that the LORD has commanded.

EXODUS 36:1

Bezalel and Aholiab were expert craftsmen because
this was what God had specifically anointed them to do.
What about you? Do you know that God has also given
you a unique gift?

You may not be able to sing like a famous gospel
singer or preach like your favorite preacher, but there is
something that you are exceptionally good at. Identify
your most dominant skill and focus on it. Paul said, "This
one thing I do" *(Philippians 3:13)*. A jack-of-all-trades is
usually a master of none.

Dominion is your divine capability. It is the special
gifting of God upon you that causes you to excel in your
chosen field of endeavor. When you find your dominion
domain, you will reign and excel in it. Your ability to
recognize and diligently develop your most dominant
skill is the first step to attaining excellence and success
in life.

The hand of the **diligent** will rule, but the lazy
man will be put to forced labor.

PROVERBS 12:24

Your skill and proficiency will eventually promote you to a place of prominence and leadership.

> Do you see a man who **excels** in his work? He will stand before kings; He will not stand before unknown men.

PROVERBS 22:29

Excellence and success in life are not just for a few people. They are for every believer in Christ Jesus. You have the dominion power to prosper and excel in the works of your hands. Strive to accomplish the best in all that you do. God has destined you to take the lead!

Remove the word *can't* from your vocabulary! With your dominion power, even the sky cannot limit you! Right now, say out loud:

I CAN be all that God has made me to be! I CAN be a success. I am not a failure. I CAN stand out and excel in all that I do. I CAN be a trailblazer. I CAN be a role model.

Yes you can! You CAN DO ALL THINGS through Christ who gives you strength. He has given you dominion power to excel, so locate your dominion domain and begin to DOMINATE in it.

The Dominion Lifestyle Is a Reality

Beloved, God has done everything to make the dominion lifestyle a reality for you. You do not have to get to heaven before you can experience a blessed and victorious life. In Christ, God has richly given us all things to enjoy right here on this earth *(1 Timothy 6:17)*! God has called every believer to enjoy blessings. He has not called us to **endure** curses!

Anything short of the dominion lifestyle is a substandard way to live. Please do not settle for anything less than the dominion lifestyle. You do not belong in the pit. You belong in the palace! Do not join the ranks of those who have settled for life on the plains.

> God has called every believer to **enjoy** blessings. He has not called us to **endure** curses!

Rise up from the valley of defeat, despair, despondency, and depravity. You belong on the mountaintop!

Put on your CROWN of glory. Release your CONQUERING power. Maximize your divine CAPABILITY. God has placed you far above all limitations. He has given you DOMINION.

CHAPTER FOUR
YOU ARE MADE FOR DOMINION

> Then God said, "**Let Us make man** in Our im-
> age, according to Our likeness; **let them have
> dominion** over the fish of the sea, over the birds
> of the air, and over the cattle, over all the earth
> and over every creeping thing that creeps on
> the earth."

> GENESIS 1:26

Of all the creatures that God made, man is the most
supreme. Every bird, mammal, and reptile that God created was made after its own kind. But the creation of
man was quite unique. Man was not created after the
likeness of any earthly being. No, he was made in the
image and likeness of the Almighty Himself. He was
created after God's kind.

It was his superior build that set him in a position
of authority and power over all of creation. You see,
there is an unmistakable connection between the
phrases: *"Let us make man in Our image, after Our like-*

ness" and *"Let them have dominion."* If Adam were not made in the image and likeness of God, he could never have had dominion in the earth.

If you take away God's image and likeness from man, he would be in the same rank as any other creature that God created. The image and likeness of God placed man far above everything that He had made. It placed him, as it were, in the class of God—a level far superior to any other created being!

You cannot separate an object's form from its function. Just as a cup is specifically shaped to hold water, so also God made man in His image and after His likeness, so that he could be a carrier or container of God's glory and power.

Only in God's image and likeness could Adam carry God's glory and power within him. And it was God's glory upon Adam that qualified him to have dominion in the earth. God **formed** Adam in His image and likeness so that he could **function** or walk in dominion in the earth.

Sadly, Adam, through his disobedience, soiled the divine image, which was given to him by God. Through his sin, Adam fell from his position of power and authority. He became deformed. He could no longer carry the glory of God. He became handicapped, powerless, and incapable of walking in dominion. Consequently, all of humanity became captive to the devil, constantly subject to every form of satanic oppression.

Today, negative situations and circumstances dominate most of humanity. Unpleasant circumstances have become so common that people, even some believers, have accepted tragedy as part of life.

Beloved, you need to know that tragedy and destruction is not life! It is death! And it is not your portion in Jesus' name.

> For I know the thoughts and plans that I have for you, says the LORD, thoughts and plans for welfare and peace and not for evil, to give you hope in your final outcome.
>
> *JEREMIAH 29:11 (AMP)*

The evil that exists in the world today is the painful result of Adam's fall. But in the beginning of creation, God made everything perfect *(Genesis 1)*. Man was created to live a sin-free life, a life that is also free from sickness, danger, and disease. God **blessed** man. He did not curse him. Man was lord and master in the earth. He had dominion, not **deprivation**. He lived in **splendor**, not **squalor**. Simply put, from the beginning, God ordained man to live in **ease**, not in ***dis-ease***!

The good news is that over 2,000 years ago, Jesus restored wholeness to the human race. Through His life, death, burial, and resurrection, He redeemed humanity from the bondage of the devil. He restored us back to the position of power and dominion that man had from the beginning. In Christ, we are made whole again. In Him we are no longer deformed. Rather, we are conformed back to the image of God.

For whom He did foreknow, He also did pre-
destinate to be conformed to the image of
His Son, that He might be the firstborn
among many brethren.

ROMANS 8:29

By virtue of your new nature in Christ, in God's
eyes, you look just like Adam did before the fall...you
look like God. You bear His image and His likeness. In

> In Christ, we are made whole again. In Him we are no longer **deformed**. Rather, we are **conformed** back to the image of God.

Jesus, God's glory and power
is restored to you. You are a
carrier of God's very presence
and His awesome power.
Christ in you is the hope of
glory (*Colossians 1:27*).

This means that you, too,
can walk in dominion just like
Adam once did: To all who
believe in Him, Jesus gives them the power, the legal
right, to reign in life as sons of the Most High God.

But as many as received Him, to them He gave
the right to become children of God, to those
who believe in His name.

JOHN 1:12

As a born-again believer, because you are born of
God and bear His image, you have been given the power
to overcome the world with all its woes.

For whatever is born of God overcomes the world. And this is the victory that has overcome the world—our faith.

1 JOHN 5:4

THE IMAGE AND LIKENESS OF GOD

Make no mistake about it, God's image and likeness, which you are fashioned after, does not refer to human bodily features such as your nose, ears, hands, and so forth. God is a Spirit (John 4:24). He cannot and should not be likened to any earthly or physical form (Deuteronomy 4:15-16).

However, the image and likeness of God in which Adam was made, and to which you are conformed in Christ, refers to the personality or nature of God. In other words, when God said, *"Let us make man in Our image, after Our likeness,"* He was simply saying, *"Let us make man to take on Our divine nature."*

When you look in the mirror, what do you see? You see your spitting image staring back at you. In like manner, God wants you to reflect Him. He made you to be an exact representation of His Person—His holiness, righteousness, truth, love, knowledge, and power.

His image and likeness basically represent all that is God—His glory, His character, and His qualities. Jeremiah 9:24 gives a very precise description of God's divine nature:

But let him that glorieth glory in this, the he understands and knoweth Me, that I am the Lord which exercise loving kindness, judgment, and righteousness in the earth: for in these things I delight says the LORD.

The Lord revealed Himself to Moses:
And the LORD passed before him and proclaimed, "The LORD, the LORD God, merciful and gracious, longsuffering, and abounding in goodness and truth."

EXODUS 34: 6

> God wants you to reflect Him! He made you to be an exact representation of His Person.

These verses reveal that God is loving and kind. God is holy and just. He is righteous in all His ways. God wants us to resemble Him in all these attributes.

He hath showed thee, O man, what is good, and what doth the LORD require of thee, but to do justly, and to love mercy, and to walk humbly with thy God?

MICAH 6:8

Just as God delights in loving-kindness, we also are required to love mercy. He delights in justice; hence we should do justly. He delights in righteousness; we must then walk humbly and uprightly with Him.

THE PROCESS OF CONFORMING

You will notice that in Romans 8:29, the apostle Paul wrote that God predestined you *"...to be conformed to the image of His Son."*

The phrase *to be* implies that conformity is a process. You do not suddenly look like Christ the day that you receive His gift of salvation. Rather you become like Him. You *"...grow up in all things into Him who is the head—Christ" (Ephesians 4:15).*

The best way I can illustrate this principle is by using the analogy of human conception. We all know that human life begins from the moment the egg is fertilized by the sperm. But consider this. Scientists tell us that an embryo is extremely tiny in size. As a matter of fact, at this stage in life, a baby in his mother's womb is smaller than a little speck of dust!

If you observe a fetus during the first few weeks and even months of conception, though he is in every aspect a human being, he does not look like a person. However the more the baby grows, the more he takes on the form and image of a human being.

When you became born again, the "seed" or "embryo" of God's nature was deposited in you (1 John 3:9). You possessed the potential to be conformed to God's likeness and image. Yet, like a fetus must keep growing to bear resemblance to a human being, so also you must keep developing in Christ in order to be conformed to

His image. If you want to look like Him, you must keep growing in your knowledge and understanding of His Word. You must keep growing in His love.

> Like a fetus must keep growing to bear resemblance to a human being, so also you must keep developing in Christ in order to be conformed to His image.

Many believers today are living defeated lives. They are not living in dominion. A major reason for this is because they are not developing in their walk with God. They are stagnant. Many are in the same spot they were when they became born again five, ten, even twenty years ago! They are still spiritual fetuses. They are not growing into Christ. They are not becoming conformed to His image.

If you refuse to grow, you will not walk in the glory and power that God has ordained for you. But the more you keep maturing and developing spiritually, the more you will look like Christ. And the more you look like Him, the more you are conformed to His image, the greater your ability will be to walk in dominion!

ARE YOU *CONFORMING* OR *COMPROMISING?*

How do you grow into Christ? How do you become conformed to His image? Well, one way is by cleaving to Him and forsaking everything that He hates. Simply put, you grow into Christ by abiding in Him and staying committed to a lifestyle of righteousness.

I am the true vine, and My Father is the vinedresser. Every branch in Me that does not bear fruit He takes away; and every branch that bears fruit He prunes, that it may

> The more you are conformed to His image ... the greater your ability will be to walk in dominion!

bear more fruit. You are already clean because of the word which I have spoken to you. Abide in Me, and I in you. As the branch cannot bear fruit of itself, unless it abides in the vine, neither can you, unless you abide in Me. I am the vine, you are the branches. He who abides in Me, and I in him, bears much fruit; for without Me you can do nothing.

JOHN 15:1-5

Through Jesus, the *Vine*, God has made the fullness of His glory and power available to you. Everything God is and has is now yours in Christ. His nature, His life, His Spirit, His faith, His love, joy, and peace all reside in you.

As His divine power has given to us all things that pertain to life and godliness, through the knowledge of Him who called us by glory and virtue, by which have been given to us exceedingly great and precious promises, **that through these you may be partakers of the divine nature, having escaped the corruption that is in the world through lust.**

2 PETER 1:3-4

As you abide in the *Vine*, as you fellowship with Him in prayer and the study of His Word, everything that pertains to life and godliness will without fail blossom and prosper in you. You will progressively grow into Christ according to the plan of God. Righteousness will naturally become your way of life.

> Blessed is the man who walks not in the counsel of the ungodly, nor stands in the path of sinners, nor sits in the seat of the scornful; But his delight is in the law of the LORD, and in His law he meditates day and night. He shall be like a tree planted by the rivers of water, that brings forth its fruit in its season, whose leaf also shall not wither; And whatever he does shall prosper.

> PSALM 1:1-3

On the other hand, the more you indulge in sin, the less you will look like Jesus. If you keep wallowing in the *mud pit* of sin, you will not grow in Christ, as you should. Instead you will be deformed. You will be incapable of exercising your dominion authority, as God wants you to.

Jesus has clothed you with a garment of righteousness. Do not soil it with sin! At conversion, you received the gift of salvation and new birth in Christ. But you have a responsibility, on a daily basis, to keep yourself unspotted, or unsoiled, by the evil in the world. It is your duty to *"walk worthy of God who calls you into His own kingdom and glory"* (1 Thessalonians 2:12).

Jesus bathed you in His blood and made you sparkling clean. Do not return like a dog to the vomit and vileness of fleshly lust. It is disgusting but it is true. Dogs actually lap up their own vomit. The next time you feel tempted to indulge yourself in an old habit, think about this: Do you really want to sit down and eat slimy, sickening *vomit*? This grim thought should help keep you away from the filthy waters of sin or carnality!

Sin is a deadly *cancer* that kills. If you keep indulging in sin, not only will you get dirty, you will also become infected by *satanic germs*. You will open yourself to intense satanic oppression and attack. You will not be able to dominate or stand against the enemy in battle. The reason why satan could never dominate Christ was because Jesus kept Himself clean. He said, *"For the ruler of this world is coming, and he has nothing in Me"* (John 14:30).

Sadly, there are some believers who take God's grace for granted. They willfully and intentionally commit sin because they know that God is merciful and there is no limit to His forgiveness.

Beloved, please understand that sin is a *demoter*. It will keep you backward when you should be pressing forward. Each time you compromise, your spiritual growth is stunted. Something *dies* within you any time you sin. If you want to walk in dominion, you must stay away from sin. Do not mess with sin. Put off the works of darkness. Then you will be empowered to exercise dominion over every negative circumstance and situation.

PART TWO

POSITION YOURSELF FOR DOMINION

But God, who is rich in mercy, because of His great love with which He loved us, … **raised us up together, and made us sit together in the heavenly places in Christ Jesus.**

EPHESIANS 2:4-7

CHAPTER FIVE

GOD HAS ALREADY ENTHRONED YOU

Though you live in the world, you are not of this world. As a son of the Most High, you are situated in the very throne room of the Almighty God. You are seated together in the heavenly places in Christ.

> But God, who is rich in mercy, because of His great love with which He loved us, even when we were dead in trespasses, made us alive together with Christ (by grace you have been saved), and raised us up together, **and made us sit together in the heavenly places in Christ Jesus.**
>
> EPHESIANS 2:4-7

Beloved, you are ordained for dominion. And your heavenly seat is not an ordinary seat—it is the seat of God's Omnipotent Power! The Amplified Bible says you have "...*joint seating with Him*..." at the right hand side of God. The word *joint* means "to share" or "to have in common." This means that you occupy an equal position of authority with Jesus. You have the same power that Jesus operated with in the earth. If no force of hell, not even death, could withstand Jesus, then no satanic force has the power to dominate or oppress you (*Luke 10:18-19*).

This is the great advantage that you have over the devil and all his cohorts. The devil is not seated together with God. You are! You are raised far above every principality, power and force of darkness. satan and all his agents are subject to you. You are not at their mercy. They are at your mercy! You have the power to keep evil under your feet.

UNDERSTANDING IS CRUCIAL

It is one thing for God to give you a heavenly seat. It is yet another thing entirely for you to take your place and sit down. God has already enthroned you. Positionally, **every** believer (not just a privileged few) has joint seating in Christ in heavenly places. As far as God is concerned, your honored seat in the heavenly places is a settled matter. It is guaranteed!

But unless you have a full understanding of your covenant position, you will not enjoy the benefits and privileges of your highly esteemed *heavenly seat.*

> A man who is in honor, yet does not understand, Is like the beasts that perish.

> PSALM 49:20

Ironically, although God has placed every Christian far above the devil and all his agents, many believers today are still being dominated and oppressed by satan simply because they lack a true understanding of their covenant position in Christ. Hosea 4:6 says, "My people perish **for lack of knowledge.**"

> It is one thing for God to give you a heavenly seat. It is yet another thing entirely for you to take your place and sit down!

Though God has ordained them to be highly placed nobles, they live like lowly paupers, in want and terrible starvation because of their ignorance.

> Therefore my people have gone into **captivity, Because they have no knowledge**; Their **honorable men are famished,** And their multitude dried up with thirst.
>
> ISAIAH 5:13

If you do not want to go into captivity, if you do not want to be "famished," if you do not want to become dried up by thirst and deprivation, you must have a full understanding of your covenant position.

When you understand the great position that you have in Christ, you will confidently occupy your seat of power. You will ascend the throne that He has prepared for you and reign as a king! Therefore, if you want to walk in dominion, it is extremely important for you to understand who you are in Christ.

AVOID AN "IDENTITY CRISIS." KNOW WHO YOU ARE!

A famous military strategist once propounded an astounding theory, which, according to him, is vital to the success of any war. He said that in battle, there are two essentials for victory: Know your enemy and know yourself.

According to him, if you know your enemy and you know yourself, you are guaranteed of 100-percent victory over the enemy all the time. But if you know your enemy but do not know yourself, or you know yourself but do not know your enemy, you would only have a 50/50 chance of winning. And if you neither know yourself nor your enemy you have absolutely no chance of victory in battle.

This theory is so true where spiritual warfare is concerned. If you neither know yourself nor your enemy, the devil, you cannot be victorious in life. Scripture clearly warns you not to be ignorant of the devil's devices (2 Corinthians 2:11). To be unaware of the enemy's strategies, mindset, and make-up is to give him an advantage or upper hand over you. God forbid that this should ever happen!

However, equally important to your victory in life's battles is your ability to know yourself. You must know who you are in Christ. It is not enough for you to know your enemy; you must also know yourself. Some people know *many* things about the devil but do not know *anything* about who they are in Christ. As a result they *magnify* the devil's deeds while the power of God in them lies dormant. This is not healthy. Many such believers have met tragic ends because of such an imbalance.

A person's ignorance gives the devil an open invitation to steal, kill, and destroy. So whenever the devil wants to bring a believer down to a low place, the first thing he does is to inflict him with what I call an *"identity crisis."* This simply means that he tries to make him unsure of his covenant position in Christ.

He knows that if he can get a Christian to be unaware of his heavenly seat, he will successfully defeat him. Remember Hosea 4:6? God's own people are destroyed *because of their lack of knowledge*. On the other hand, it is absolutely impossible for satan to conquer a Christian who is full of faith and fully conscious of his identity in Christ.

The devil's sinister strategy of trying to bring a person down through an *identity crisis* is vividly demonstrated on two occasions in Scripture. First, it is seen at the dawn of human history, when satan tempted Eve in the Garden of Eden. Here, he tricked Eve into believing that the reason why God did not want Adam and Eve to eat the fruit of the tree was because He did not want them to be like God.

Yet, if Eve had really known who she was, if she had been sure of her covenant position in God, she would never have fallen for the devil's lie. She would have known that she did not have to be like God *because... she was already like God!* God made her in His exact image and likeness.

Sadly, because she lacked a full understanding of her God-given identity, she (along with her husband, Adam) fell from the position of honor that God had given her. She was defeated hands down by the devil.

Thousands of years after that incident, satan used the same sinister scheme against the Lord Jesus. Twice, the devious devil attempted to make Jesus doubt His identity when he said to Him, *"If you are the Son of God...."*

Now, keep in mind that only a few days prior, during His baptism, God had affirmed Jesus' identity in the presence of many witnesses. God had declared Jesus to be His Beloved Son in whom He was well pleased. Yet, almost immediately, satan tried to inflict the Lord with an identity crisis by bombarding Him with thoughts of uncertainty and doubt.

However, unlike Eve, Jesus did not buy into the lie of the devil. He simply could not be fooled. He was sure of His position with the Father. He knew that He and the Father were one. God had called Him "My Beloved Son," and He had no doubts about it. He believed and held on to God's affirmation of Him. He did not fall for the devil's tricks. As a result, satan had to flee in disgrace from the presence of our Lord *(Matthew 4:10-11)*. You see, the devil simply cannot withstand a person who knows his covenant position in Christ.

Deception thrives on ignorance. It is impossible for satan to confuse or deceive you when you are armed with the Truth. When you fully understand your covenant position in Christ, it will be absolutely impossible for the devil to overthrow or bring you low by an identity crisis. He will not be able to devour or destroy you.

In the midst of life's trials and temptations, you must always know your position. You must get your *bearing* right. According to the Word of God, you are seated in heavenly places, far above the turbulence of life. So do not allow your present circumstance or situation to define your position.

Yes, you may have failed in times past. But that does not mean you are a failure. You may lack finances now, but that does not mean you are a poor person. You may be facing a health challenge right now, but according to the Word of God, you are not weak or sickly. No! You are strong. Beloved, you are not who the devil says you are … you are who God says you are!

Do not lose sight of your *spiritual bearing*. Keep your heavenly position in focus. You are seated far above all principalities, powers, and limitations of the earth. No matter what is going on in the world around you, remember that you are securely located in heavenly places. You are seated jointly with the God of the whole universe.

Just imagine the implications of this. In a very real sense, you are a right-hand man of God. You have all the power of the universe at your disposal. The problems of the earth simply cannot bind you.

When you know how powerful you are in Christ, you will use God's power to your fullest advantage. You will soar above all the turbulences and tribulations of life. You will be strong and well-positioned to face the enemy with full force. You will subdue all his attacks with great precision and accuracy. You will strike at the devil and never miss your target. You will dominate him and every circumstance that he brings your way. Every force of hell will be subject to you.

Beloved, do you know who you are in Christ? Are you fully aware of your covenant position in Him? When the devil floods your mind with fears and doubts, do you fall for his lies or do you stand sure and secure in your God-given identity?

If the enemy has tried to bring you low with an identity crisis, please fall on your knees for a moment and be liberated today by the words of this prayer:

In Jesus' mighty name, I command every scale of deceit and ignorance to fall off from your eyes. I command every satanic "smoke screen" to be destroyed! I command your eyes of understanding to become enlightened. Henceforth you will no longer be ignorant. But you will know who you are. You will gain a clear and full knowledge of your covenant position. Receive wisdom to occupy your heavenly seat. In Jesus' most powerful name, amen!

THE FOUR "LEGS" OF YOUR COVENANT SEAT

While on the Isle of Patmos, John the Revelator had a privileged glimpse into the throne room of God. There he beheld something incredibly awesome:

And immediately I was in the spirit: and, behold, a throne was set in heaven, and One sat on the throne…

Before the throne there was a sea of glass, like crystal. And in the midst of the throne, **and around the throne**, were four living creatures full of eyes in front and in back. The first living creature was like **a lion**, the second living creature like **a calf**, the third living creature had a face like **a man**, and the fourth living creature was like **a flying eagle**.

REVELATION 4:2, 6-7

Not only did John see the Lord seated in majesty upon His throne, but he observed something else. He saw four living creatures that were continually worshipping the Lord. The first creature looked like a lion, the second like a calf, the third had a face like a man, while the fourth creature looked like a flying eagle.

Interestingly, these four beings, which are also positioned around God's throne, symbolize four very key aspects of your covenant position in Christ. In four plain words they simply, yet strongly, describe who you are in Christ.

1. You are a sheep (calf).
2. You are a lion.
3. You are a son.
4. You are an eagle.

Of all the animals mentioned in scripture, the lion, sheep, and eagle feature most prominently as symbols. There are about 23 references to the eagle, 84 references to the lion, and the sheep is mentioned about 183 times. This bears testimony to the immense significance and importance of these animals.

Another unique fact is that all three creatures are used in direct reference to the Lord. In Deuteronomy 11:32, God is likened to an eagle in the way that He cared and led His chosen people, Israel. In Isaiah 53:7 and John 1:29, 36, Jesus is described as the Lamb of God who was slain for the sins of the world. Last but not the least, in Revelation 5:5, He is called the Lion of the tribe of Judah.

It is not surprising that these animals, which Scripture uses to help reveal God to us, also help you understand who you are in Christ. In the following chapters we will discuss in detail how the description of these creatures—the lion, sheep, eagle, and of course man—all correspond and relate to your covenant position in Christ. From our analysis, you will better understand who you are in Christ. You will reign in life. You will be empowered to walk in absolute dominion.

Chapter Six

You Are a Sheep

… The second living creature like a calf…

REVELATION 4:7

The word *calf* is another name for *lamb*, which is a young sheep. Of all the four aspects of your covenant position in Christ, your position as a sheep of God is the most fundamental. Unless you first establish yourself as a sheep of God, you cannot operate as a son, lion, or eagle.

The sheep position, more than any other, best depicts your redemption in Christ. Remember, the redemption that you have in Christ is what actually qualifies you for dominion in the earth. Before Jesus gave you the dominion authority to rule and reign in the earth, He **first** redeemed you.

> And they sang a new song, saying: "You are worthy to take the scroll, and to open its seals; For You were slain, and have **redeemed us to God** by Your blood out of every tribe and tongue and

people and nation, and have made us kings and priests to our God; and **we shall reign on the earth.**"

REVELATION 5:9-10

You simply cannot reign if you are not redeemed. Jesus first redeemed you to God and then made you a king, and *because of your* redemption, you shall reign in the earth…you shall have dominion!

It therefore follows that, unless you first establish yourself as a sheep of God, unless you are redeemed by the blood of the Lamb, you will never be able to walk in dominion. This is why I have made the sheep position my first focus.

Your salvation qualifies you for every blessing that is available to you from God. Without redemption in Christ, the promises and power of God are far beyond your reach. But while you were still lost in sin, Jesus, the Lamb of God, took the punishment for your sins and brought you back to God.

> Now may the God of peace who brought up our Lord Jesus from the dead, that great Shepherd of the sheep, through the blood of the everlasting covenant, make you complete in every good work to do His will, working in you what is well pleasing in His sight, through Jesus Christ, to whom be glory forever and ever.
>
> *HEBREWS 13:20-21*

Jesus bore the punishment for your sin. He then sought you and found you. He redeemed you to God by His blood, which perfects and makes you eligible to reign in dominion.

THE LORD IS YOUR SHEPHERD

Dominion in life is simply not possible without the leadership of Jesus, the Great Shepherd of the sheep. Psalm 23 is one of the most popular chapters in the Bible. Almost every Christian is familiar with the words of this great song of David. Yet, relatively few actually know the full implication of its profound opening verse,

> The LORD is my Shepherd [to feed, guide, and shield me], I shall not lack.
>
> PSALM 23:1 (AMP)

Unless you first establish yourself as a sheep of God, one who is redeemed by the blood of the Lamb, you will never be able to walk in dominion.

This statement powerfully describes, in a nutshell, the dominion that you have as a sheep of God. You see, dominion can only be exercised in a state of abundance. God made this clear right from the beginning when He gave man dominion authority in the first place. In Genesis 1:28, God clearly associates abundance with dominion when He said, "*Be fruitful and multiply; fill the earth and subdue it; have dominion.*" God unmistakably expected Adam and Eve to exercise their dominion in a state or environment of fruitfulness and wealth, not in an atmosphere of lack.

It is absolutely impossible for a person who is impoverished to exercise dominion. Proverbs 22:7 says, *"The rich rules over the poor, and the borrower is servant to the lender."* Who rules? The rich! Who is in subjection? The poor! Here you can see it in black and white: The rich rule while the poor are enslaved. The rich walk in dominion, while the poor walk as servants.

> Dominion in life can only be exercised in a state of abundance.

The scriptural principle of the rich ruling over the poor is so evident in today's world. You would observe that the wealthiest nations are the ones that play a major role in the overall political climate of the world. Without question, the richer a nation is, the greater its influence would be in the world community.

On the other hand, poorer nations do not enjoy such privileged power. They have little or no clout in the decision-making *arena* of world affairs. More often than not, they are left to *dance to the tune* of their more affluent counterparts.

> The rich man's wealth is his strong city; the destruction of the poor is their poverty.
>
> PROVERBS 10:15

Make no mistake about it: The rich do rule over the poor. China, for instance, is considered to be one of the fastest growing economies in the world today. Because of its current financial *explosion,* it is also regarded as an emerging world power. Moreover, the world's greatest super power, the United States of America, is also the world's wealthiest nation. This goes to prove that wealth and authority, riches and power, go hand in hand. The rich rule. They have dominion! Those who have abundance will always be masters over those who are in lack.

So as a sheep of God, your dominion is assured because the Lord is your Shepherd and you shall not lack. In Him you have abundance in all things. You are in the best position to exert your dominion authority in every circumstance of life.

The Lord is your Shepherd; you shall not lack. You will not know lack of *any* kind. This means that you are rich. You are not poor. You will not lack the power that you need to be *above* in life. You will never be beneath. You are not a servant to the circumstances and trials of life. You are qualified to rule and reign. Simply put, when the Lord is your shepherd, you will walk in dominion.

Your position as a sheep establishes you in the inexhaustible, overflowing, abundant provision of God. He is absolutely in charge of your protection, provision, direction, and defense. Your riches in Christ empower you to have dominion in life. Under His leadership, you will be fed, guided, and shielded. You will enjoy a life of supremacy and victory over every circumstance. You will never know defeat. Remember, the rich rule! And who are the rich? They are those who have no lack—those whose Shepherd is the Lord.

From the Amplified Bible's Version of Psalm 23:1, you would observe that Jesus, the Great Shepherd, performs three main functions for His sheep. (1) He feeds them; (2) He leads (or guides) them; and (3) He shields them. Let us briefly examine each function in closer detail.

THE SHEPHERD FEEDS YOU

He makes me to lie down in green pastures.

PSALM 23:2A

Sheep are extremely helpless creatures by nature. They are totally dependent upon their shepherd for sustenance. Many other domesticated animals can make it on their own. But not so with sheep! Sheep rely heavily on their shepherd for their daily provision of food, water, and other necessities. Without nourishment which comes from the shepherd, sheep would have little or no chance for survival. They plainly depend upon the shepherd to meet their **every** need!

As a sheep of God, you must realize that you can do nothing, absolutely nothing, apart from Jesus, your Great Shepherd. Really, without Him, you are totally helpless. You simply cannot do anything for yourself. You must depend upon Him absolutely to meet your every need *"for in Him we live and move and have our being"* (Acts 17:28).

God knows how completely incapable you are without Him. This is why He is fully committed to meeting all (not some, but all) your needs. Without Him you can do or have nothing. So He makes you lie down in green pastures where H*e supplies "all your need according to His riches in glory by Christ Jesus" (Philippians 4:19).*

Did you see that? Your needs are supplied according to God's riches by Christ Jesus, your Great Shepherd. In His green pastures, Jesus feeds you to the fullest. There, all your wants—spiritual, physical, material, financial, and so forth—are met over and beyond what you can ever imagine. Just name your need. He is able and willing to meet it.

Sadly, many sheep of God do not understand how weak and incapable they are. They try to make it on their own, without the Shepherd's supply. They run in vain from pillar to post; from one relative to the other; to their employer, creditor, and so forth trying to meet their needs by human strength and wisdom.

Please do not get me wrong. God does use human beings as channels or distributors of His abundant supply. But it is important that you never forget that people are no more than mere channels. They are not the source of supply. God is the Source—the only Source!

Friend, you need to understand that the help of man is vain. If you make man your source, you will be totally disappointed. The pastures that human wisdom and ability offer are not green at all. They are dry, brown, barren, fruitless places. Only the Shepherd's pastures are green, lush, and fruitful. Only His provision truly satisfies.

I discovered a long time ago that God alone is my true Source. He is my Supplier! Others are just His channels of blessing. Employees, your employer is not your supplier. Wives, your husband is not your supplier. Entrepreneurs, your clientele are not your suppliers. Only God is. Only He can supply all your needs. Quit trying to meet your needs by yourself. Trust Him completely for your *supplies*.

Whenever you have a need, talk to God about it first. He knows what you need even before you ask Him. Come unto Him with all your worries, needs, and burdens. In exchange He will give you rest. He will make you lie down and relax in His green pastures. He will supply all your need.

Only the shepherd knows where the pastures are green. Allow Him to lead you to His chosen *channel* of blessing. That *channel* may be a business idea or dream. In obedience to the Shepherd's voice, step out in faith and pursue that dream or idea. Follow through with it. Or it may be a divine connection with a person who will give you your dream job. Fill out that job application. And when you are employed, be the most diligent person in the company. Then the Shepherd will make you fruitful and prosperous in life.

When you know that the Lord is your shepherd, you will know that you are not *on your own* in this world. Do not look to another to be fed, or else you will remain hungry and needy. Jesus, your Shepherd is 100-percent responsible for you. He is your Source. He is committed to supplying all your needs according to His riches in glory. You are His dependent son, His ward, His charge...His offspring and He is totally committed to your welfare and upkeep.

THE SHEPHERD LEADS YOU

> He leads me beside the still waters. He restores my soul; He leads me in the paths of righteousness for His name's sake.

> PSALM 23:2A-3

Of all the animals in the animal kingdom, sheep are one of the least intelligent. Quite plainly, sheep are shockingly dumb! In a very real sense, sheep do not have a mind of their own. They cannot think for themselves. They must depend absolutely on the shepherd to think for them. They need him to make right decisions. They need the shepherd to lead them.

Unlike most other animals, if a sheep gets lost, it is incapable of finding its own way back home. A sheep cannot decipher between safety and danger. If one sheep wanders off and falls off a cliff, the other sheep in the flock, in their characteristic "herd mentality," will follow suit without discerning the danger.

Obviously, to make it in life, sheep desperately rely on the shepherd to lead them in the way that they should go. The shepherd is well aware of the *intellectual incompetence* of his sheep, and so with his staff, the shepherd lovingly guides his sheep in the right path.

It may sound so humbling but it is true. As far as God is concerned, compared to His wisdom, you are no more intelligent than a sheep. The foolishness of God is wiser than men, and the weakness of God is stronger than men (1 Corinthians 1:25). You need to get this, and you will forever be delivered from a prideful spirit. You will be inspired to always remain humble before God. You see, *you* are not really as *smart* as you think. In **God's eyes, you are mentally incapable of navigating your own way through life**.

Jeremiah 10:23 says, *"O Lord, I know the way of man is not in himself; It is not in man who walks to direct his own steps."* It is not in you, it is not in your own human wisdom, to direct your own path. You need the Shepherd to lead and guide you every step of life's way. You desperately need His guidance in your career, marriage, and all your decisions without exception.

One of the greatest killers of destiny today is the spirit of presumption. A believer who is ruled by presumption takes action without acknowledging or consulting God. He does not rely absolutely on Him for guidance. While he may consult God on some issues, he selectively leaves Him out on others. This is foolish, dangerous, and wrong.

Remember, like sheep, you are incapable of making good judgments on your own. You cannot decipher between safety and danger; good and bad. In your human eyes, there is a way that seems right, but God knows that it ultimately leads to death. So you must trust your Shepherd with all of life's decisions or choices.

Trust in the Lord with all your heart, and lean not on your own understanding; In all your ways acknowledge Him, and He shall direct your paths. Do not be wise in your own eyes....

PROVERBS 3:5-7A

The Shepherd must be allowed to lead you step-by-step, moment-by-moment, in every single aspect of your life. He is the Only Wise God. It is not enough to have a *good idea*. You must have a *God idea*! The wisest human idea is but foolishness to the God whose ways and thoughts are far higher than man's. 1 Corinthians 3:19 says, *"For the wisdom of this world is foolishness with God."*

Like sheep, you simply cannot make it on your own. To go through life without the Shepherd's leading is to court disaster. This is why presumptuous believers, no matter how good and logical their assumptions are, often fall off the dangerous cliffs of life. Their destinies become abruptly shattered.

Good decisions are just not good enough! You need God-decisions, choices that are inspired by the leading of the Lord, to secure a life of victory, prosperity, and dominion. You dare not go through one moment without His specific direction guiding you. Like sheep, you need your Shepherd to help you find the right paths in life. What may seem right to you is wrong to God. Allow Him to lead you.

If you want to experience still waters and peace, if you desire restoration, you must submit yourself completely under the authority and leadership of your Great

Shepherd. You must be led by Him and not by your human instincts. Human wisdom will lead you to fall off dangerous cliffs in life. Though many think they are *smart* enough to lead their own lives, their best efforts will only end up in futility.

Only the path outlined by God will lead to fullness and fruitfulness in life. Peace and prosperity is guaranteed when the Shepherd is allowed to lead. He will lead you beside still, peaceful waters. He will restore and refresh you. He will give you double for your trouble. He will restore to you all that the enemy had stolen. Blessed be His name forever!

THE SHEPHERD SHIELDS YOU

> Yea, though I walk through the valley of the shadow of death, I will fear no evil; For You are with me; Your rod and Your staff, they comfort me.
>
> *PSALM 23:4*

Sheep are extremely timid creatures. They are so fearful that their own shadows scare them! When confronted with danger, sheep have no means of defending themselves. Lions have strong, deadly claws; snakes have venomous fangs that deliver fatal bites; elephants have tusks to gore enemies to death, but sheep… well, sheep have nothing. They have no in-built weapons to combat their enemies. They are awfully vulnerable animals.

The best that sheep can do in the face of an attacker is to run frantically and unreasonably in any direction. Truly without the shepherd, sheep would be *goners*! They would have absolutely no chance for survival. This is why one of the shepherd's principal duties is to save and protect his sheep from enemies. A shepherd's commitment to the safety and preservation of his sheep is so strong that he would gladly risk his life to save any of his sheep.

Remember David, the shepherd boy? On two different occasions, he bravely put his life on the line when a bear and a lion threatened the lives of his flock (1 Samuel 17:34-35). As far as David was concerned, he would rather die than to allow a bear or lion to devour any one of his sheep.

Well, our Lord Jesus is even greater than David. He is the Greatest Shepherd of all! He is the Good Shepherd who laid down His life for you to prove how much He cared for and values His sheep.

> I am the good shepherd; and I know My sheep, and am known by My own. As the Father knows Me, even so I know the Father; and I lay down My life for the sheep.
>
> JOHN 10:14-15

Prior to Christ's sacrifice, all of mankind was like wayward sheep gone astray from God. But Jesus, the Great Shepherd, sought and redeemed man back to God through the sacrifice of His life. *"All we like sheep have gone astray; We have turned, every one, to his own way; And the Lord has laid on Him the iniquity of us all"* (Isaiah 53:6).

Truly, like sheep, without the protection of your Good Shepherd, you are extremely vulnerable. You have absolutely no means of defending yourself against the one who seeks to steal, kill, and destroy you. In short, without the protection of your Shepherd, Jesus, you would be a *goner* in life. You would be meat for the enemy's consumption. It is only by the mercy of your Good Shepherd that you are not consumed. You are spared from being the devil's prey!

Now, a shepherd uses both his rod and staff to guard and protect his sheep. In some countries, the staff is a firm, long wooden stick that he uses to guide the sheep and keep them in the right path. But in other places, the staff is a short, chubby stick (similar to the shape of a baseball bat) with nails or sharp objects attached to it. He uses this nail-studded weapon to attack, kill, or ward off wild beasts from devouring the sheep.

Like shepherds in the natural, Jesus your Good Shepherd is truly your Minister of Defense. Because you are His sheep, He has taken it upon Himself to contend, or fight against, any enemy that should ever come against you.

> But thus says the LORD: "Even the captives of the mighty shall be taken away, and the prey of the terrible be delivered; For I will contend with him who contends with you, and I will save your children. I will feed those who oppress you with their own flesh, and they shall be drunk with their own blood as with sweet

wine. All flesh shall know that I, the LORD, am your Savior, and your Redeemer, the Mighty One of Jacob."

ISAIAH 49:24-26

He is your Shield and Defender. He is solidly committed to your protection and preservation. Living in this world, where tragedy and evil abound, is really like walking through the valley of the shadow of death. But always remember, in the midst of all the danger that surrounds you, that you are not alone. Your Shepherd is always walking with you. He is with you *"as a mighty terrible one: therefore your persecutors shall stumble, and they shall not prevail: they shall be greatly ashamed; for they shall not prosper: their everlasting confusion shall never be forgotten"* (Jeremiah 20:11). No evil can devour or dominate you under your Good Shepherd's watch. Alleluia to Jesus, the Great Shepherd and Bishop of your soul!

STAY IN HIS SHEEPFOLD

Customarily, sheep live in a sheepfold, or sheep pen. Each morning the shepherd leads his flock out to green pastures where they can eat grass. After the sheep have eaten the grass in one place, the shepherd brings them to a new pasture. He also leads them to the streams of water so that they can drink and be refreshed (Psalm 23:2).

To dwell safely, sheep must remain under the wise and watchful guide of their shepherd. They must remain in the sheepfold! Like I mentioned earlier, sheep cannot defend themselves against wild animals.

On your own, you do not stand a chance against the enemy. However, as long as you abide in Christ, as long as you stay in His sheepfold, you cannot be taken prey by the devil. He is the Good Shepherd who keeps His sheep safe and secure in His arms.

In Christ, you are securely positioned in His fold where He will keep you safe in the midst of a dangerous and wicked world. Yet, to enjoy the covering of the shepherd, the sheep must remain solely dependent upon the guidance of the shepherd. Remember, dominion is not possible without the leading of Jesus, the Great Shepherd.

Sadly, there are many Christians today who through presumption, sinful lifestyles, or disobedience to the Shepherd's voice, have strayed away from His sheepfold. As a result, they have opened themselves up to intense danger and satanic attack. They experience one defeat after another. They are not walking in dominion.

Please understand that you cannot confidently claim God's promise for protection if you constantly disregard His instructions. If a sheep veers away from the protective sanctuary of its shepherd and foolishly goes off into the wild, he is bound to fall to danger.

If you are reading this book today and you know that you have gone astray, I have good news for you: Do not despair because your Shepherd still cares. Do not believe in the lies of the devil when he says, God will no longer have anything to do with you because you have fallen into one sin or the other. That is not true! God's love for you is unconditional. Even now, in your backslidden, prodigal, or complacent state, you are still important to Him. You are extremely valuable to your Shepherd, and He wants you back!

> What do you think? If a man has a hundred sheep, and one of them goes astray, does he not leave the ninety-nine and go to the mountains to seek the one that is straying?
>
> MATTHEW 18:12

In the natural, it is typical for some sheep to stubbornly veer away from the rest of the flock. At such times, the shepherd uses his rod to bring such *wayward* sheep back home. The rod is commonly known to be a long wooden stick that is slightly curved at the top end.

Using the curved end of the rod to encircle the sheep's head, the shepherd then draws the rebellious sheep back to himself. The rod here is symbolic of God's Word. Any time a believer arrogantly strays away from God's way, God uses the rod of His Word to correct and discipline him. He does this to bring His sheep *back in line*. With the rod of His Word, He delivers them from a sinful and damaging lifestyle.

The Shepherd greatly values His sheep. He does not want to lose any believer to sin or destruction. He wants us all to remain in His sheepfold because that is where our safety and dominion is guaranteed.

> You cannot confidently claim God's promise for protection if you constantly disregard His instructions!

So whenever you do err from His path, He will send the rod of His Word to you. He will speak to you through your pastor, other believers, Christian resources, and above all His Word—the Holy Scriptures.

When you hear His word of correction and discipline, do not arrogantly resist it. Do not give excuses for your sinful and prodigal behavior. Rather submit yourself to His *Rod*. Humbly bow yourself in repentance and let the rod of God's Word *encircle* your head. Let it bring you back to God.

> My son, do not despise the chastening of the LORD, nor be discouraged when you are rebuked by Him; For whom the Lord loves He chastens, and scourges every son whom He receives.... Now no chastening seems to be joyful for the present, but painful; nevertheless, afterward it yields the peaceable fruit of righteousness to those who have been trained by it.
>
> *HEBREWS 12:5-6, 11*

As you submit to the chastening rod of God's Word, He will forgive you, and you will be restored. You will walk His path of holiness once more. You will dwell in His sheepfold where the enemy can do you no harm.

So, if you want to enjoy the Shepherd's protection, if you want to walk in dominion, you must stay in His sheepfold. In Psalm 91, David calls it the *secret place*.

He who dwells in the secret place of the Most High shall remain stable and fixed under the shadow of the Almighty [Whose power no foe can withstand].

PSALM 91:1(AMP)

When as His sheep you abide in His secret place, you will be preserved. You will never be devoured. You will be protected from the *wild beasts of life*. If the enemy dares to attack or assault you, he will have to face your Shepherd Jesus first. Needless to say, he cannot stand a chance against the Lord. This is God's ironclad guarantee for your protection!

Chapter Seven

The Profile of a "Sheep" Christian

At this point, I feel that it is necessary to draw your attention to the fact that not every self-professed Christian is really a sheep of God. Just because you come to church regularly, even serve in one capacity or the other, does not mean that you are part of His flock. Jesus Himself testified that not every one who calls Him "Lord, Lord," truly belongs to Him. Make no mistake about it: The Lord knows those who are truly His!

If the truth is to be told, many congregations worldwide today do not just consist of sheep. They also include a mixed multitude of goatish or bull-like people. How then can you become a true sheep of God? According to John 10, true sheep of God are those who do two things. First, they hear God, and second, they obey God's voice.

> But he who enters by the door is the shepherd of the sheep. The watchman opens the door for this man, and the sheep **listen to his voice and heed it**; and he calls his own sheep by name and brings (leads) them out. When he has

brought his own sheep outside, he walks on before them, and **the sheep follow him because they know his voice**.

JOHN 10:2-4

You will notice that Jesus did not just say that the sheep listen to their shepherd's voice. He also said that they *pay attention* to it. If God speaks to you and you do not obey Him, you are not a sheep Christian. Instead, I am sorry to say, you are a stubborn, arrogant goat! And Jesus is the great Shepherd of sheep. He is not obligated to goats, rams, dogs, or bulls.

> Sheep do not lead the Shepherd. It is the shepherd who leads the sheep!

Now, a sheep is probably one of the meekest and most domesticated animals on earth. It humbly follows the leading of its shepherd. As the Lamb of God, Jesus Himself was described as humble, meek, gentle, and totally submissive to the Father's will.

> He was oppressed and He was afflicted, yet He opened not His mouth; He was led as a lamb to the slaughter, and as a sheep before its shearers is silent, so He opened not His mouth.

ISAIAH 53:7

He opened not His mouth. This means that He did not contradict or go against the Father's plan. He chose to follow only the path that God had mapped out for Him. He chose to do the Father's will instead of His own.

If you claim to be a Christian, but you are stubborn and rebellious to God's voice, you are not His sheep. You cannot confidently claim that He is your Shepherd if you go through life without seeking His counsel or submitting to His will. True sheep of God hear God's voice and obey Him continuously.

> True sheep of God are those who do two things—
> (1) They hear God, and
> (2) They obey God's voice.

LET THE SHEPHERD LEAD YOU

There are many so-called Christians who do not live like God's sheep. They behave more like bulls and goats! They are arrogant and strong-willed. They constantly ignore or disregard God's voice. If you desire to be God's sheep, you must choose to walk humbly with Him.

Sheep do not lead the Shepherd. It is the shepherd that leads the sheep! And it is not possible to follow God's leading without possessing a spirit of humility. Humility implies the total submission of your will to the Lord.

If you are frequently in the habit of disregarding God's instruction, please stop that practice now. If you want to walk in dominion, you must learn never to ignore or treat God's Word lightly. Determine to make hearing and following God your lifestyle. This was how the Lord

Jesus lived His earthly life. He never took a step without a direct instruction from the Father. This is how you must live, too!

> I can of Myself do nothing. As I hear, I judge; and My judgment is righteous, because I do not seek My own will but the will of the Father who sent Me.
>
> *JOHN 5:30*

Your ability to hear God is extremely crucial when you are at a major crossroads in your life, when you are at a junction where there are no *middle roads*. There are only two ways—God's way or man's way. God's way will lead to life—promotion, prosperity, peace, and progress. Man's way leads to death—destruction, disappointment, and demotion. At such points in your life's journey, any decision that you take will make a major and lasting impact on your destiny—for good or for bad.

At this point in life, one wrong move may even cost you your entire destiny! If you refuse to hear or obey God's voice, you may forever live in regret and shame. Remember Esau? One careless decision at a crucial cross-roads in his life cost him his destiny. No amount of lamentation could salvage what he had lost. Tears of regret could not restore his birthright to him (Hebrews 12:16-17). However, if you seek God's counsel and listen to His voice, you will be launched into the fullness of God's purpose and plan for your life.

In early 1998, I was at such a point in my life. One sunny Sunday morning during worship service, as I was making my way to the altar, the Holy Spirit compelled me to stop for a moment. Standing upon the gallery He prompted me to scan through the entire auditorium, which at this time was filled with worshippers. The church was so jam-packed that some people had to sit on the staircases.

Then He said, *"Look and see. This is the greatest that this house will experience under your leadership. Your time in this commission is over. I am about to change the seasons of your life. You must leave. You dare not stay a moment longer. If you do so, you will no longer have my backing and you will become a liability."*

I honestly wish that I can tell you that after He spoke, I was so excited that I felt like packing my bags and leaving the next day. But the truth of the matter is that humanly speaking, it was not a very easy instruction to follow. God had asked me to resign at a time when in my own eyes I was about to enjoy the fruit of my labor.

For five years, with the help of the Holy Spirit, we had built the church from *scratch*. In the early days of the church's inception, I even went without a salary. Now God was asking me to leave at a time when things were pretty good. With joy I had watched the church grow in leaps and bounds. We had labored and built, and now it was time to *enter into our rest*. Yet according to God's timeline for my life, **that was not the time of *rest*. It was the time of *release*!** He was about to launch me into the fullness of my destiny.

> Not only will your ability to hear and obey God's voice get you to your place of destiny, it will also keep you there!

Beyond any shadow of doubt, I knew that it was God speaking to me. I realized that I had two options. I could either disobey God by refusing to leave my comfort zone. Or I could obey Him and step out in faith into the *unknown*. I am glad to say that against my human feelings, I chose to obey God. As a result, He catapulted me into a depth and fullness of my life's assignment that I had not known before. I really begin to walk in the fullness of my destiny. I am glad to say that I have not for one day regretted my decision to obey His voice. He has made my life and ministry extremely rewarding and fulfilling.

The best place to be is in the center of God's will. Not only will your ability to hear and obey God's voice get you to your place of destiny, it will also keep you there. I hate to imagine what the outcome of my life would have been if I did not hear or obey God's voice at such a crucial time in my life. I owe the dominion and favor that I continue to enjoy in my life entirely to His leading.

Beloved, living by every instruction from God's Word will guarantee your dominion in life. Dominion is just not possible without the leadership of the Shepherd. You must learn, every day, to both hear and heed the voice of God concerning every matter of life. If you desire to be a true sheep of God, if you want to walk in never-ending dominion, you must choose to live by God's Word alone.

Chapter Eight
Hearing God is a Must

Contrary to the experience of many believers today, God is not a silent introvert. He is an extrovert! He is a vocal God. And He has so much to say to you. Just as He spoke through His prophets in times past, He is constantly speaking to His people today.

> God, who at various times and in various ways spoke in time past to the fathers by the prophets, has in these last days spoken to us by His Son, whom He has appointed heir of all things, through whom also He made the worlds.

Hebrews 1:1-2

Without question, God *is* speaking, but are you listening? According to Webster's dictionary, the word *listen* is a verb that means "to make a conscious effort to hear." This implies that it takes more than wishful desire to hear God. It requires a great deal of deliberate determination on your part. You must make a disciplined effort to hear God's voice.

As a rule, God speaks to His people through His Word. God will never say anything that is contrary to what He has already said in the Scriptures. Therefore, if you want to hear God, you must make conscious and deliberate efforts every single day to study the Word of God. The more you study the Scriptures, the greater your ability will be to discern His voice.

This is where many Christians encounter problems. They find it difficult to hear God speak to them because they are pathetically lazy when it comes to Bible study. The only time such Christians read the Word of God is during a church service. And yet they expect to hear God's voice!

Please note that I used the word *study*. To effectively hear God's voice, you must not just read His Word casually. You must study it *intently*.

> **Study** to shew thyself approved unto God, a workman that needeth not to be ashamed, **rightly dividing the word of truth**.
>
> *2 TIMOTHY 3:16 (KJV)*

It takes more than wishful desire to hear God. It requires a great deal of deliberate determination on your part.

Devote all your energies to knowing and understanding God's Word. God's Word has something specific to say about every aspect of your life. There is no need for you to ever be in a state of dilemma or confusion. Refer to God's Word for direction in life. Determine never to act on your own initiative. Do not be presumptuous.

WHY YOU MUST HEAR GOD

Andrea Crouch once sang, *"We need to hear from You; we need a word from You; if we don't hear from You, what will we do? Loving You more each day, show us Your perfect way; there is no other way that we can live."*

These lyrics beautifully summarize why you need to hear God every single moment of your life. If you do not hear from God, you would not know what to do! You would be utterly lost and confused. In short, you would be in no position to live a life of power and victory. Remember: Dominion is only possible when the Shepherd is allowed to lead. Jesus said, *"Man shall not live by bread alone, but by every word that proceeds from the mouth of God"* (Matthew 4:4).

Life is a journey that has only been completed by God. He knows the end from the beginning. He is the Alpha and Omega. Only He knows the exact paths that lead to life and fulfillment.

> O Lord, I know the way of man is not in himself; It is not in man who walks to direct his own steps.
>
> JEREMIAH 10:23

So if you want to live a life of dominion and power, you must allow Him to lead you in the way. You must rely on Him to help you navigate life's course. When you acknowledge Him, He will direct and guide you by His voice.

> Trust in the LORD with all your heart, and lean not on your own understanding; In all your ways acknowledge Him, and He shall direct your paths.

> *PROVERBS 3:5-6*

Now, there are three major voices in the earth to-day—the voice of God, the voice of man, and the voice of the devil. Of all three, only God's voice is genuine and authentic. Only His voice will get you to your desired haven of peace and prosperity. You must learn to know His voice so that the enemy will not take you off the track of your destiny. Without daily direction from God, your life will most definitely shipwreck. There is a way that seems right but the end is death. It is only God's way that leads to life.

Are you at a crossroads in your life? Please do not take any step without specific instruction from God's Word. Acknowledge Him in all your ways. Let Him direct your paths. Open your heart daily to hear His instruction. Be led of Him. Do not go ahead of Him!

Sadly, some people come to God after they have already made up their minds about what it is they have decided to do. They do not come seeking God for guidance. Rather they come asking Him to endorse their own manmade choices. This is wrong! Do not *inform* God of your decision. Let Him tell you what to do. Consult and acknowledge Him first in all of your ways.

Though God has a special plan for every man and woman on the surface of the earth, it is only those who keep hearing and obeying God who will ever live

> Be **led** of God. Do not go **ahead** of Him!

to fulfill their divine purpose. You need the constant direction of God's voice for your great destiny to come to fruition. Without His direction, you can never get to your destination in life.

> There is a way that seems right to a man, but its end is the way of death.
>
> PROVERBS 14:12

Those who chart their own path and disregard the shepherd's leading eventually get devoured. Their destinies become abruptly shattered. Yours will not be shattered in Jesus' mighty name!

God's way may not make sense to your human reason, but I guarantee you, it is the way to go. If you want to make any headway in life, if you want to accomplish great things, you must make up your mind not to be led by your own *common sense*. Instead, choose to always be led by *God's sense*. Walk by faith, not by sight.

Common sense is *common*. It will only bring you to mediocre and average places. But if you want to ride on the high places of the earth, if you want to live in the realm of the extraordinary, you must choose to rely on God's Holy Spirit for direction in life.

In 1996, the church that I pastored was barely one year old when the Lord gave an instruction, which seemed totally *illogical* to my human mind. He said, "Leave this facility and move to a bigger one." As far I was concerned, this did not make sense. We were still in our *infancy* stage, especially where numerical growth and finances were concerned. Our rent of $700 was just what we could afford at the time. Moreover, our services were not what you would call "jam-packed." It did not seem as if we had outgrown the building. I did not see why we should move.

> Promotion, prosperity, and provision in life are guaranteed when God is allowed to lead the way!

Yet, I heard God say emphatically, "It is time for you to leave this place." Quite frankly, I am embarrassed to admit that I did not have the courage to obey God promptly. However, while I was *dragging my feet* on the matter, I heard God's voice again. This time He spoke firmly and with greater urgency: "I have asked you to move out of this place and look for another facility. Why are you hesitating? If you delay any further, I will do through another church what I originally planned to do here." This was unmistakably my *wake-up* call. I certainly did not want another person to take my place in destiny. Without further delay, I began to look for another property.

To cut a long story short, the Lord led us to a facility with a monthly rent of $3,000. This was more than four times what we were paying in our old place! But I am glad to say that God did not fail us. (God never fails!) Our $3,000 rent was always paid on time.

What's more, from that point on, the church experienced phenomenal growth. Friends, promotion, prosperity, and dominion in life are guaranteed when God is allowed to lead the way.

Therefore hearing God for divine guidance is your greatest asset for walking in dominion. Hearing God makes the dominion lifestyle possible. If you cannot hear Him, you cannot walk in dominion. It is as simple as that!

YOU CAN HEAR HIS VOICE EVERY DAY

As a sheep of God, you are entitled to hear His voice every day. In John 10: 2-4 *(quoted earlier)*, the Lord, speaking from the experience of Middle Eastern shepherds, vividly illustrates how natural and simple it is for His sheep to know and hear His voice.

You see, sheep have an amazing ability to recognize their shepherd's voice. In those times, it was typical for different shepherds to share one common sheepfold where they would keep all their sheep at the end of the day. They would then appoint a gatekeeper or porter to lock and guard the sheep pen through the night. Then in the morning, the shepherds would return to call out their respective flocks.

> Hearing God for divine guidance is your greatest asset for walking in dominion.

Remarkably, though their different sheep had been inter-mingled, the sheep would only respond to the voice of their own individual shepherd. They would not respond to another shepherd's call. By this example, Jesus simply states that if a mere sheep (*which, by the way, is not considered to be a very intelligent animal*) can discern and follow its own shepherd's voice, how much more should the sheep of the Most High God be able to do so?

Friend, it is not a hard thing for you to know the voice of God. He is your Father; you are His child. Honestly, is it hard for a child to hear his own parent's voice? Absolutely not! God has blessed my wife and me with three wonderful children. None of them had to be *gifted* before they could know and recognize our voices. Their ability to discern our voices came quite natu-rally to them. It was a potential inbuilt in them by the Creator God.

It is that way with you where hearing God is con-cerned. Hearing God is not a special *gift* that is reserved for the privileged few. It is not only for pastors, those in ministry, the *popular* men and women of God. On the contrary, it is the covenant right of every son and daugh-ter of the most High God.

Just as it is normal for my children to recognize my voice, and for sheep to know and pick out their shepherd's voice, it's normal for every Christian to hear God's voice. The ability to discern the voice of God is inbuilt inside of you because you are God's offspring. On the contrary, it is very abnormal and unnatural for a believer not to be able to hear from God. Like a sheep in the natural, you should know the voice of Jesus, your Good Shepherd. You should be able to distinguish His voice from that of the stranger.

Yet many believers complain that they do not know the voice of God. They have trouble identifying the voice of God from other voices. As a result, they rely on others to *hear* God for them. They go from one prophet to another to receive a "word" from the Lord.

While God, from time to time, may speak to you through others, He still wants you to be able to hear Him for yourself. You are His child, and you are entitled to hear your Father speak directly to you every single day of your life.

LEARNING TO HEAR GOD'S VOICE

While it is true that every believer has within them the capability to discern the voice of God, you must realize that it is your responsibility to develop your innate ability until it reaches its full potential. It is only then that you would actually enjoy hearing the voice of God frequently and fluently. The sheep of Jesus follow Him because they have come to *"know His voice,"* not by chance, but by choice!

Knowledge is basically a function of learning. Everything that you know today has been acquired through the learning process. Learning is the stepping-stone to knowledge.

It therefore follows that if you desire to know God's voice, you must take the time to learn it. The reason why many believers have trouble discerning God's voice is because they have not taken time to know His voice through learning. Learning is not something that happens by chance. If you want to learn anything, you must choose to on purpose.

> The sheep of Jesus follow Him because they have come to *"know His voice,"* not by chance, but by choice!

According to psychologists and educators, one of the most powerful and effective ways of learning is through repetition. You have a very high chance of understanding a concept and retaining it in your memory if you are repeatedly exposed to it.

In this regard, the answer to the question, "How can I know the voice of God?" is quite simple. It is the same way a baby learns the voice of his mother—through repeated exposure. It is said that a baby can recognize his mother's voice right from the womb!

> God's voice is not learned by accident. It is learned by acquaintance!

From the time of conception, until he is weaned, a child spends almost all his time with his mother. Her voice is the one that he hears over and over again. So a child who frequently hears his mother's voice eventually knows it so well that he can single out his mother's voice among a crowd of women.

Similarly, God's voice is not learned by *accident*. It is learned by *acquaintance*. The more you spend time with God, in prayer and the study of His Word, the more acquainted you will be with His voice. The more you remain in God's presence, the more accustomed you will be to His voice. Remember, *hearing God for divine guidance is your greatest asset for walking in dominion!*

CHAPTER NINE

KEYS TO HEARING GOD CONTINUALLY

The Lord God has given Me the tongue of the learned, that I should know how to speak a word in season to him who is weary. He awakens me morning by morning, He awakens my ear to hear as the learned.

ISAIAH 50:4

Some people think that you only need to hear God on the *major* issues of life. However, if you desire to walk in dominion, you need to hear God *morning by morning*. You must always be *awake* to His voice. You must be certain of His will in all matters of life. Acknowledge Him in all (*not some*) of your ways. Nothing is too trivial!

Remember, you are mentally incapable of navigating your own way through life. You must rely absolutely on your Shepherd to lead and guide you every step of life's way. You desperately need His guidance in all your decisions without exception.

There is a way that seems right, but it is not right! Your own way, no matter how smart or logical it seems to be, will most definitely lead to death. Only God's way brings dominion in life. This is why you need to hear God's voice directing you in your normal day-to-day activities, the same way you would seek His guidance when you want to make a major life decision such as the choice of a career or a spouse. We will now examine what you must do to be led by God on a moment-by-moment basis.

1. HAVE A CONSTANT DESIRE TO BE LED.

What you do not desire, you do not deserve. If you do not expect to be led of God, you will never hear His voice. To hear God's voice and enjoy His direction in life, you must value His counsel to the extent that you are willing to give your entire being to seeking His will alone in all things.

The proof of desire is pursuit! You will never find what you do not seek. If you want to hear His voice, you must make a conscious choice to seek His counsel. Some people seek God's leading in some things while they refuse to consult Him on other issues.

If you desire God's leading, you must never be tired of seeking counsel from Him. *Trust in the LORD with all your heart, and lean not on your own understanding; In all your ways acknowledge Him, and He shall direct your paths (Proverbs 3:5-6).* You must deliberately acknowledge Him in all your ways. This means that you must desire His will and His way alone.

God does not lead by force. He leads by your free will. As you continually and willingly give up control of your life to the Lord, you will surely hear His voice. The more you desire the Spirit's leading, the more sensitive you will be to His voice.

> The proof of desire is pursuit! You will never find what you do not seek.

Often times when people complain about prayer being hard, the real truth of the matter is that they are not desperate enough for God. But when you have a strong desire for God, you will not be able to contain yourself. You will long to come into His presence. You will not seek Him because you have to. You will seek Him because you really want to!

Beloved, are you willing to set aside your personal agenda and embrace God's will alone? Are you willing to *burn all your bridges* and put away all your *alternatives* and say, "It is either God's way or no way"? If you can sincerely answer 'yes' to these questions, then you can rest assured that you will hear God clearly on all issues of life. You will never ever be confused again.

2. SEEK GOD IN PRAYER.

Call to Me, and I will answer you, and show you
great and mighty things, which you do not know.

JEREMIAH 33:3

Where can God's voice be heard? Where does He reveal the answers to every question of your heart? Where does He make known His will?

In the room of prayer!

Have you ever been in a situation in which you felt *stuck* in life? When it seemed as if your plans, dreams, and aspirations all came to a standstill? When you thought that you could neither go backward nor advance forward? What a worrisome place to be! Well, in 1995, I found myself in this *deadlock-like* condition.

I had just relocated to the United States to take up a pastoral assignment in Dallas, Texas. For me, moving to the U.S. was more than just accepting a job transfer. It meant taking a step toward the fulfillment of the word which God spoke to me in 1987: *"Thousands upon thousands of people are roaming the streets of America as sheep without a shepherd. I am sending you to be their undershepherd while I remain the Chief Shepherd."*

I consequently *burned all my bridges* to answer destiny's call. I gave away my cars, possessions, and valuable assets and said goodbye to the place that I had called home for thirty years. I knew that there was no turning back.

However, when I arrived at Dallas, I soon discovered that things were not exactly what I had expected. At one point, it seemed as if I would have to *face reality*, and look for a secular job *to keep body and soul together*.

The fact that my new bride was expecting our first child added to my concern. It seemed as if all my dreams and aspirations suddenly came to a screeching halt! *What must I do?* I thought. Going back to Nigeria was definitely out of the question. But then I wondered, *What is the way forward?*

At a time like this, God's voice is truly a Christian's best asset. This is because nothing ever takes Him by surprise. Nothing is hidden from His eyes. He knows exactly what must be done in every circumstance of life. He is the Great Way-Maker. The Good Shepherd goes ahead of His sheep in life's journey to make every crooked way straight (Isaiah 45:2).

He says in Isaiah 42:16, *"I will bring the blind by a way they did not know; I will lead them in paths they have not known. I will make darkness light before them, and crooked places straight. These things I will do for them, and not forsake them."* Yes, He is the only One who knows the way through the wilderness. All we have to do is to follow!

So I chose not to succumb to the mounting pressure from human reason. I decided instead to seek God in prayer. As I prayed, He gave me direction. God spoke so clearly and definitely to my heart. He told me point blank—*"Do not look for a secular job! I called you in 1991 to be My full-time minister. Do not carry out My job on a part-time basis! I am still able to pay your bills. I can take care of you, your wife, and the child that is to be born. I did not send you to the United States to suffer. I am not a demoter. I am a promoter! If you remain focused on the work of My kingdom, if you refuse to be distracted, I will be with you. I will exalt you and establish you in this land.*"

After God spoke, I had incredible peace. I chose not to be moved by the circumstances that faced me. I was confident that God was in control and He was making a way for me. A few months later, God opened a door for me to plant a church in Houston. Since I moved to Houston, my ministry and life has gone from one level of glory to the next. I have never had to take on a secular job to sustain my family and me. God keeps blessing me beyond my wildest imagination. And I give Him all the glory!

Please note that, in the room of prayer, worship and praise must be given top priority. Always begin your time of prayer by offering God high quality praise. As you worship Him and make Him your main focus, you will discover that even before you make your request, He will begin to speak to you. When you rejoice before God in your heart, and songs of praise are on your lips, He will cause you to hear His glorious voice (Isaiah 30:29-30)!

For every fiery trial of life, God has a divine escape route. He has a way of escape. When you ask Him in prayer, He will lead you in the way of deliverance and victory. Whenever you are in doubt or confused, inquire from God what to do.

Do not worry or fret about troubling circumstances. Instead call upon the Lord in prayer. Ask God direct questions. Ask Him about your present situation. Ask Him about the future. He will tell you exactly which way to go. Never worry. Always pray!

3. FAST.

Sometimes it will become necessary for you to combine fasting with your prayer. Anytime you pray and it seems as if you are not hearing God clearly, reinforce your prayers with fasting. Contrary to what some believe, fasting does not change God. Fasting changes you! It makes you more open and receptive to His voice.

Fasting is the process whereby you "starve" your sensual appetites to feed your spirit man. As this occurs, you will become more alert to the realm of the spirit than the natural realm. As a result, you will be in the best position to receive *signals* from heaven. Your spiritual ears will become more in tune to God's voice.

Typically, there are three kinds of fasts:

* **Absolute Fast**: This is when a believer completely abstains from water and food. Advisably, the longest a person should ever go without drinking water is three days. *Acts 9:9*

> Fasting does not change God. Fasting changes you! It makes you more open and receptive to His voice.

* **Normal Fast**: When a person abstains from food, but drinks water, the fast is called a normal fast. In a normal

fast, a person may choose to abstain from food. However, he still drinks lots of water. The human body is made up of about 70 percent water. So it is extremely crucial to our survival. Ideally, three days is the maximum a person may do without water. However, you may abstain from food alone for a much longer period.

- **Partial Fast**: Finally, in a partial fast, a believer abstains from certain kinds of foods for a period of time in order to seek God. Typically, in this kind of fast your meal may mainly consist of fruits, nuts, or vegetables. Pleasant delicacies such as meat, fish, and sweets are excluded from your diet. *Daniel 10:2-3*

No matter the type or length of your fast, to get the best results, you must give ample time to seeking God in prayer and searching out His counsel in His word. Fasting done in a right way will always open your spiritual eyes and ears to God's leading.

This is a truth that my wife can happily testify to. Before she accepted my marriage proposal, she went on a two-day absolute fast. Though she had been praying on the matter for quite some time, she wanted to be "super" sure that I was God's choice before she said yes.

She had already faced two disappointing experiences with previous suitors and she desperately wanted to *get it right* this time. So she sought God in prayer and fasting for two days, eating no food and drinking no water. By the end of the second day she knew God's counsel for sure. God literally spoke *volumes* to her and confirmed beyond any shadow of doubt that I was *the* one!

Do you need direction? Have you been praying but it seems as if you are just not hearing His voice? If so, please do not give up in frustration. Do not resort to human alternatives. Instead, take a few days to separate yourself unto the Lord in fasting and prayer. You will surely hear Him loud and clear. Guaranteed!

4. BE WATCHFUL.

Often you may not hear God's instruction the first time that you pray. This is especially true about major decisions. However, if you really want to be led of Him, you must be willing to wait on Him for as long as you have to.

> I will stand my watch and set myself on the rampart, and **watch to see what He will say to me.**
>
> HABAKKUK 2:1B

The phrase "watch to see" conveys the image of a guard or watchman who is steadfastly keeping watch at his position. He allows nothing and no one to take him away from his post. If you desire to hear God's voice, you must be ready to stay in His presence. This means that you will determine not to make any move until you hear Him speak.

Many Christians do not hear God's voice because they are not *watching*. They are *wandering*. They claim to seek God, but at the same time, they are running helter-skelter in search of *alternative* solutions. Their minds and hearts are not 100 percent fixed on Him.

"Watching" and "waiting" on God implies that you separate yourself from all the noises and babblings of the world. You cut off the voices of worldly opinion and reports of man and choose to focus only on God. You meditate upon His Word alone.

> Many Christians do not hear God's voice because they are not "watching." They are "wandering"!

Hastiness and hyperactivity are sound barriers that tend to impair a person's ability to hear God's voice. Daily, you need to observe a time of total separation unto God if you desire to develop and maintain a high level of sensitivity to His voice. Do not be in a hurry when you are seeking His counsel in prayer. Do not take any step in life without a clear word from the Lord.

Beloved, profound visions and heavenly insights are delivered during watchful moments. This is why Jesus said, "Watch and pray." If you want to pick up signals from heaven, if you want to stay tuned to the Holy Spirit's frequency, you must be an established and committed watchman! To hear God, you must be prepared not only to pray but also to watch and wait patiently upon Him.

Are you at a crossroads in your life today? Do you desperately need God's direction? Well, rather than gamble with a range of manmade *solutions*, I encourage you to take time out to wait upon the Lord. Cease from your activity and be still before Him. As you do, God will speak. Your spirit will commune with the Spirit of God, and you will hear His voice clearly. He will direct your every step. *Your ears shall hear a word behind you, saying, "This is the way, walk in it." Whenever you turn to the right hand or whenever you turn to the left (Isaiah 30:21).*

HOW YOU CAN BE SURE OF GOD'S VOICE

Earlier on, I mentioned that there are three voices in the earth: the voice of God, the voice of man, and the voice of the devil. To avoid confusion, it is very important that you understand how to distinguish God's voice from the others.

Many believers have heard their own voice and have erroneously felt that it was God leading them. Others, because they lacked discernment, have even listened to the devil.

I am sure that you cannot count how many times you have heard the phrase, "God said to me..." But, do not be deceived, not every "word" is from the Lord. So how can you be sure that the voice that you are hearing or the prophetic words from other believers are actually God's? Well, here are some helpful indicators:

1. GOD'S VOICE IS BACKED BY GOD'S WORD.

God's spoken word will always agree with His written Word! This fact cannot be overemphasized. God will never say anything to contradict biblical principles, precepts, or precedents. Whatever you hear—whether by prophecy, by your personal study of God's Word, in your spirit man, or by an au-

> God will never say anything to contradict Biblical principles, precepts, or precedents.

dible voice—must be tested and proven by God's Word. Any voice that does not align with Scripture, no matter how convincing, must be rejected immediately.

2. GOD'S VOICE WILL BRING PEACE TO YOUR HEART.

God's voice will always resolve your inner conflicts. His voice puts an end to turmoil. God is the God of peace. He is not a God of confusion!

> I will hear what God the LORD will speak, for He will speak peace to His people and to His saints; but let them not turn back to folly.

> *PSALM 85:8*

God speaks peace, not chaos. Any word or thought that adds to or heightens confusion is not of God. On the contrary, God's Word brings solutions. His voice will answer your questions beyond any reasonable doubt. His voice will settle every matter and put an end to every troubling thought or emotion.

3. GOD'S VOICE BRINGS EASE AND COMFORT.

God is not a nag. He is an Encourager and an Edifier. The voice of God, even when He is reproving or rebuking you, will always bring comfort. It is not burdensome or grievous. Whatever God says to you will draw you near to Him. It will not drive you away. His words will always encourage you to boldly approach His throne. He will never fill you with guilt, shame, or fear. Rather, God's voice will always bring you close to His warm embrace.

4. GOD'S VOICE WILL BRING JOY AND FILL YOU WITH HOPE.

The leading of God is always accompanied with joy. Now please understand that this is different from happiness. *Joy* is based on *Jesus* while *happiness* is based on *happenings*. You know that you have heard from God when what you have heard fills you with unshaken hope in Jesus even in the midst of a hopeless situation. His voice will make you excited and full of faith in the midst of a storm. This is more than a feeling of euphoria. God's voice brings joy, which in turn strengthens your faith. In this sense, God's voice brings divine strength. His voice empowers.

5. GOD'S VOICE WILL MOVE YOU FORWARD.

Any voice that directs you back to the failures and frustrations of the past is not of God. The leading of God is always *progressive*. It is not *retrogressive*. God's voice will move you forward. It will not take you backward. In this sense God's voice is always accompanied by promotion and prosperity.

> Who is the man that fears the LORD? Him shall He teach in the way He chooses. He himself shall dwell in prosperity, and his descendants shall inherit the earth.
>
> PSALM 25:12-13

You know that you have heard God when you gain fresh insight into your situation to propel you forward. Yes! God's voice sheds light on dark situations. His voice opens doors and makes a way where there seems to be no way.

TEST EVERY WORD!

Beloved, do not believe every spirit, but test the spirits, whether they are of God; because many false prophets have gone out into the world.

1 JOHN 4:1

In conclusion, please understand that you have a responsibility to test every voice that you hear. Put every word that comes to you under the scrutiny of the aforementioned indicators.

As you do, you will never again mistake the stranger's voice for God's. You will always be confident and sure when God speaks to you. You will be in a position to follow His leading alone. You will not hear strange voices. You will only discern God's voice and follow in the path that He leads. His path establishes you in the dominion lifestyle!

CHAPTER TEN

ADD OBEDIENCE TO YOUR HEARING

O come, let us worship and bow down; Let us kneel before the LORD our Maker. For He is our God, and we are the people of His pasture, and the sheep of His hand. Today, if **you will hear His voice: "Do not harden your hearts, as in the rebellion**."

PSALM 95:6-8A

It is one thing for you to hear God's voice. It is yet another to obey Him. I have met many believers who claim to hear God, yet for reasons best known to them, they repeatedly choose not to follow His instructions. If you pride yourself with the fact that you can hear God but you do not act upon His word with quick and prompt obedience, then your hearing is in vain. Such disobedience is nothing short of prideful rebellion. It is an evil and abominable sin.

For rebellion is as the sin of witchcraft, and stubbornness is as iniquity and idolatry.

1 SAMUEL 15:23

In John chapter 10, Jesus did not just say that His sheep hear His voice. He also said they **follow** Him. "Hearing" without "following" is incomplete. You must both hear **and** follow. Anytime God speaks to you, you must understand that He is not giving you an opinion to consider. He is giving you a commandment to obey! "If you will hear His voice: 'Do not harden your hearts.'" Do not be rebellious.

If you are a sheep Christian who walks in humility before God, you will obey Him. Jesus' meekness and humility was clearly seen in His unrivaled obedience to the Father's will (*Isaiah 53:7*). So do not just seek to understand what God's will is. More importantly, choose to walk steadfastly in it. Do not just hear God. Obey Him, too!

> Anytime God speaks to you, you must understand that He is not giving you an opinion to consider. He is giving you a commandment to obey!

Has God given you an instruction lately? Beloved, please obey without delay. Do not just obey—obey instantly. Do not fool around! Someone once said, "Delayed obedience is disobedience."

In the journey of life, Jesus, your Great Shepherd, must be your leader. You must be His follower. Follow Him alone. Do not follow fleshly wisdom or instinct. Do not pay attention to the devil's lies, either. Give no regard to the *strange* voices of fear, doubt, pessimism, or unbelief. Let only what you hear as a sheep determine whatever step you would take in life. This way your dominion will be guaranteed.

When God is leading you along a particular way, remember that He has already gone ahead of you to break every barrier and make adequate provision for you.

> I will go before you and make the crooked places straight; I will break in pieces the gates of bronze and cut the bars of iron. I will give you the treasures of darkness and hidden riches of secret places, that you may know that I, the LORD, Who calls you by your name, am the God of Israel.
>
> ISAIAH 45:2-3

Like I said, the problem with a lot of Christians is not that they are not hearing God speak, but rather, they are blatantly refusing to do what God has asked them to do. If you are the type that resists or disobeys His instruction or His leading, you are not a true sheep of God. You have shifted from His protective sanctuary and any wild *beast* can come and attack you.

> If they obey and serve Him, they shall spend their days in prosperity, and their years in pleasures. But if they do not obey, they shall perish by the sword, and they shall die without knowledge.
>
> JOB 36:11-12

If this sounds like you, please stop reading for a moment. Fall on your knees and repent right now. Beloved, disobedience has tragic consequences while obedience has great rewards. Yes, disobedience to God's voice can be deadly. It can cost a believer his destiny, sometimes even his life!

I once heard of a precious man of God whose disobedience cost him his life. He had been scheduled to travel for a preaching engagement outside the country. However, prior to the time he was to leave, he had a strong urgency in his spirit that he should cancel his trip.

Being so accustomed to God's voice, the pastor knew that it was God telling him not to travel. But when he thought of the planning and preparation that must have been done in organizing the meeting, he decided to go ahead with his original plans. Unfortunately, on his way, his plane crashed. He perished and never got to the meeting after all.

After his death, it was discovered that he had expressed to a close relative about how strongly he had felt that God did not want him to go on that trip. Misfortune befell him, not because he lacked God's instruction, but because he did not obey His voice. It was a sad and tragic end to a man who still had so much to offer the world and the body of Christ.

In 1996, against God's direct instruction, I buckled under the pressure of my pastor friend and accepted his preaching invitation to minister overseas. It was only by the mercy and grace of God that my disobedience did not result in tragic consequences.

My disobedience brought me great heartache. First, on the very night that I arrived, a gang of about twenty armed robbers invaded my mother-in-law's home. Even more fearful was the fact that my ten-month-old son was with her at the time! Thankfully, because of God's miraculous intervention, no one was hurt.

However, as if all that I had been through was not enough, when I returned back to the States, I had a lot of upsetting issues awaiting me at our church at the time. I greatly regretted my disobedience. I faced unnecessary troubles because I did not obey God. I also suffered great loss. So, I resolved never again to listen to man's voice at the expense of God's. I determined to obey God daily.

Beloved, not every open door is a God-opened door. No matter how lucrative and promising an opportunity or prospect may seem, if you have any inclination that God is not in it, turn back immediately. Do not go

> Disobedience to God's voice brings regret. Obedience to God's voice brings rewards!

against God's voice. Do not succumb to the pressures from man. Do not walk by sight. Obey God alone. Disobedience to God's voice brings **regret**. Obedience to God's voice brings **rewards**.

Troubles and tragedy of life can be avoided when you hear and obey His voice always. But if you do not follow His direction, you will rob yourself of all dignity, honor, favor, and prosperity.

So whose voice will you follow in life—the stranger's voice or God's? Any voice apart from the Spirit of God is a strange voice. As we have discovered, it does not pay to follow any other but God. You dare not follow the voice of a stranger. To do so inevitably brings gloom and doom.

YOUR OBEDIENCE MUST BE COMPLETE

There are some who obey God only when it is convenient. However, if you want to experience dominion in life, you must obey God in full. Do not obey Him in "half measures." As a matter of fact, you cannot exercise your dominion authority over the enemy if your obedience to God is not complete.

> And being ready to punish all disobedience when your obedience is fulfilled.
>
> *2 CORINTHIANS 10:6*

For every path or journey in which God will lead you, He has a series of instructions, which must all be followed. You must determine to obey God till the end, not just partially. Obey Him every step of the way. Go with God all the way, not halfway.

In the book of 1 Kings chapter 13, there is a very interesting account that rightly illustrates this point. It is the story of a mighty prophet of God, whose partial obedience brought him to a very tragic end. He had obeyed God but only to a limited degree.

The first instruction God gave him was to go to Bethel. Verse 1 clearly states that he went out of Judah to Bethel "by the word of the Lord." When he got to Bethel, God gave him another instruction. God spoke to him to prophesy against the altar. He promptly obeyed.

Then, as he was about to leave the altar and continue on his way, the king, King Jeroboam, invited him to come home with him and even promised to give him a "fat" reward. However, he flatly refused because he said, *"For so it was commanded me by the word of the LORD, saying, 'You shall not eat bread, nor drink water, nor return by the same way you came'"* (verse 9). And so in obedience to God's clear word of instruction, he chose to go another way and did not stop. So far, he had obeyed every instruction that the Lord had given unto him. But, sadly, that would soon change.

On his way, he met an old prophet who lived in Bethel and had heard about what God had done through him. The old man decided to invite the prophet from Judah over to his house for lunch. At first, the prophet declined the invitation just as he did to King Jeroboam. However, after being lied to and pressured by the old prophet, he disobeyed God and went ahead to eat at the old prophet's house.

While he was still eating at the table, God sent a prophecy against him. Ironically, the old prophet who had deceived him into disobeying God was the one who gave the prophecy. God judged him saying, *"Because you have disobeyed the word of the LORD, and have not kept the commandment which the LORD your God commanded you, but you came back, ate bread, and drank water in the place of which the LORD said to you, 'Eat no bread and drink no water', your corpse shall not come to the tomb of your fathers"* (verses 21-22).

True enough, the prophet from Judah met a very tragic and untimely end. Along the way, he was killed and devoured by a lion. The old prophet buried him in Bethel. Just as the prophecy had said, he was not buried among his own people. What a sad end to a great man. He had obeyed God, but only to a certain point. He did not obey Him to the end.

Because his obedience was not complete, he did not live to enjoy the fruit of his labor. His destiny was cut short. This is fearful indeed.

Beloved, do not pride yourself with the fact that you obey God sometimes. Strive to obey Him all the time and in all things. Just as it is possible for you to always hear God, it is possible to obey Him in full. Like you saw in the story of the prophet from Judah, partial obedience is just as bad as outright disobedience. The consequences of obeying God partially and disobeying Him are practically the same.

The late Dr. Lester Sumrall once made a profound statement that keeps inspiring me in my determination to faithfully obey God's voice. Before he passed on to be with the Lord, Dr. Sumrall once said that in sixty-three years of ministry, he had never been out of God's will …not even once! Like Jesus, he would seek God's counsel in all things and obey Him to the full. Sadly, he also noted that there are some who are so arrogant and stubborn that they have not been in the will of God one single day of their lives!

I have made my choice to take my position as a sheep Christian…to do nothing except as He commands. I will go nowhere except as He leads. And when He gives the commandment, I will carry it out to the fullest.

This is a time of sober reflection. Ask the Holy Spirit to search your heart and bring to your remembrance any instruction of God that you have ignored or not fully obeyed. Often, believers face tough times because, at some point in their lives, they have disregarded God's direct instruction. Retrace your steps. God will forgive you. The way forward, the way out of your dilemma, is to make a fresh commitment to obey God in all things.

> Partial obedience is just as bad as outright disobedience. The consequences of obeying God partially and disobeying Him are the same!

Friend, walking in dominion is only possible through a life of absolute reliance upon and obedience to God's voice. Knowing what He is saying all of the time is the secret of all winners. There will be no crisis when He is leading.

ARE YOU GOD'S TRUE SHEEP?

Like I said at the beginning, there are many "goats" and "bulls" in the church today. Yes, they faithfully attend worship services, week after week. Some even "serve" God in one capacity or the other. They prophesy and work miracles in the Lord's name. But they are not His sheep.

God knows those who are truly His. And on that Great Day of reckoning, the *pretenders*, those who lived their entire lives *playing* church, will be in for a big surprise. To such people the Lord will say, *"I never knew you; depart from Me!"*

> "Not everyone who says to Me, 'Lord, Lord,' shall enter the kingdom of heaven, but he who does the will of My Father in heaven. Many will say to Me in that day, 'Lord, Lord, have we not prophesied in Your name, cast out demons in Your name,

and done many wonders in Your name?' And then
I will declare to them, 'I never knew you; depart
from Me, you who practice lawlessness!'"

MATTHEW 7:21-23

Those who give no regard to God's word have no place
in the Shepherd's fold. Walking and living in the full understanding of your covenant position as a sheep of God
requires that you hear and obey God's voice on a consistent
basis.

> If you want to walk in dominion, you must be sensitive to God's voice and quick to obey Him!

God enthroned you as His
sheep because He knows that
you are absolutely incompe-
tent to determine the right
path for your life. You are
mentally incapable of navigating life's course. But the
journey of life becomes great
and victorious when God is allowed to lead the way.

Then it came to pass, when Pharaoh had let the
people go, that God did not lead them by way
of the land of the Philistines, although that was
near; for God said, "Lest perhaps the people
change their minds when they see war, and return to Egypt."

EXODUS 13:17-18

Note that God did not lead the Israelites through a short-
cut or *logical* route. God's way is different and higher than
man's. His way may seem to be longer but it is **the only
way** that leads to life and fulfillment. All other ways, no

matter how short, logical, and easy they may seem, will only lead to frustration, pain, and defeat. Shortcuts usually lead to dead ends!

Are you a sheep of God? Is Jesus truly the Lord and Savior of your life? Are you living a life that is totally submitted and surrendered to God's will and way? Are you daily conforming to Christ's image, or are you compromising? Can you honestly say you have been hearing and obeying God continually?

If you cannot sincerely say that you are God's sheep, though you have claimed to be a Christian for quite a while, now is the time to get real with God. Your days of *playing church* are over. Go to the Lord in prayer right now. Say, *"Lord, I am a lost sheep and I want to come back to You. Make me Your true sheep, one who hears and obeys You continually. Draw me back to Yourself and never let me go. Keep my heart humble and submitted to You. Open my ears to hear Your voice. Make my heart willing to do Your will.* ***Make*** *my feet quick and swift to obey You in all things. And all the days of my life I will follow You, my Good Shepherd. In Jesus' name I have prayed, amen!"*

Perhaps you are reading this book and wondering, *Well, I am not even a born-again Christian. I have never once been a sheep of God.* Well, I have good news for you, too. Today, right now, you can become His sheep. It does not matter what you have done or where you have been, the Good Shepherd died for you. He redeemed you and today you can become His very own. Remember, you cannot reign in life or walk in dominion, if you are not redeemed. So, if you want to be saved and delivered from the power of sin, if you want to live the rest of your life as a true sheep of God, fall on your knees right now, and pray:

Dear Lord God, I confess that I am a sinner. I desperately need Your love and forgiveness. I believe that You paid the penalty for my sin. I believe that You are the Good Shepherd who gave Your life to save me from my sins. I thank You for Your great love. From this day on, I submit my entire life to You. Please be the Savior and Lord of my life. I yield my life to You in total surrender. Help me to follow You faithfully as Your true sheep, all the days of my life. In Jesus' name, amen!

You are now ready to reign in life! You have taken the first and most crucial step necessary for walking in dominion. You have taken your position as a sheep of God! As we go on to examine the remaining three aspects of your covenant position always keep in mind that the foundational key to a life of absolute dominion lies in your ability to hear and obey God. Remember, if you want to reign in life, you must first be redeemed. If you want to walk in dominion, you must first be a true sheep of God who is sensitive to His voice and quick to obey Him. It is only from this basis that you can prosper as a lion, son, and eagle of God.

Chapter Eleven
You Are a Lion

The first living creature was like a lion…

Revelation 4:7

By virtue of your redemption, in Christ, you are not only a sheep, but you are also a lion. You are seated in heavenly places in Christ, who is the Mighty Lion of the Tribe of Judah! (*Revelation 5:5*).

In the natural realm, it is an indisputable fact that the lion is the king of the beasts. No other creature can contest the might and majesty of the lion.

> There are three things which are majestic in pace,
> Yes, four which are stately in walk: A lion, which
> is mighty among beasts and does not turn away
> from any.

Proverbs 30:29-30

A lion is feared and respected by all animals. None can harass or threaten him in the wild. He does not turn away from any other creature. He does not cower in the face of danger. Rather, he is confident and stately in his stance. He walks in majesty, dignity and power. He is in control.

Similarly, as a lion of God, you have been given indisputable authority and power in the earth. When you understand this, you will know that like a natural lion, you are mighty! As a result, you do not need to turn away from **any**—from **any** troubling situation, **any** challenge, or **any** force of the enemy!

Do not be afraid of satan or his evil attacks. It is he who ought to be afraid of you! You do not have to run away from him. Rather, it is he who must run away from you. Through dominion in Christ, you have the power to put satan and all his cohorts to flight. You are not a victim in life. You are a victor. You are a terror to the devil. You are a force to reckon with.

As an offspring of Jesus, you are also a spiritual descendant of the lion-like tribe of Judah.

> Judah, you are he whom your brothers shall praise; Your hand shall be on the neck of your enemies; Your father's children shall bow down before you. Judah is a lion's whelp; From the prey, my son, you have gone up. He bows down, he lies down as a lion; And as a lion, who shall rouse him? The scepter shall not depart from Judah, nor a lawgiver from between his feet, until Shiloh comes; And to Him shall be the

obedience of the people. Binding his donkey to the vine, and his donkey's colt to the choice vine, he washed his garments in wine, and his clothes in the blood of grapes. His eyes are darker than wine, and his teeth whiter than milk.

GENESIS 49:8-12

In this regard, Genesis 49:8-12 reveals the following key points about your covenant position.

As a lion of God:

YOU ARE THE HEAD AND NOT THE TAIL.
Judah, you are the one whom your brothers shall praise; your hand shall be on the neck of your enemies; your father's sons shall bow down to you (verse 8).

The lion is popularly known as the king of the beast. As a lion of God, you are also a God-appointed king in the earth. You have been elevated to a position of divine authority and power. You are ordained to *stand out* and be distinguished among mankind.

As a lion of God, seated in Christ in heavenly places, you are also ordained to take dominion over every force of darkness. Interestingly, a lion suffocates or strangles large prey by clamping down on the prey's neck. Then to prevent his victim from breathing, the lion places his large powerful paw over the animal's nose and mouth till it dies.

Like the lion, your hand shall be on the neck of your enemy—satan. When you come against him in your dominion authority, every negative circumstance that he throws against you will be crushed. By God's mighty hand at work in you, you are empowered to bring him down and keep him under your feet. You are destined to rule and reign over every satanic oppression.

YOU ARE THE DEVIL'S PREDATOR. HE IS YOUR PREY!

Judah, a lion's cub! With the prey, my son, you have gone high up [the mountain]. He stooped down, he crouched like a lion, and like a lioness—who dares provoke and rouse him? (verse 9).

In the natural world, the lion is the king of all predators. As a matter of fact, lions are among an exclusive class of animals called "apex predators" or super predators. This means that in the wild, they are at the top of the food chain. As a result, they are not typically preyed upon by other animals.

Similarly, as a "lion of God," you are the devil's super-predator, and *he is your prey*. Where life's battles are concerned, you are at the top of the *food chain*. You are not food for the devil's consumption. It is the enemy that is *bread* for your consumption (*Numbers 14:9*). Alleluia!

YOU ARE A LEADER AND A PERSON OF DISTINCTION.

The scepter or leadership shall not depart from Judah, nor the ruler's staff from between his feet, until Shiloh [the Messiah, the Peaceful One] comes to Whom it belongs, and to Him shall be the obedience of the people (verse 10).

Lions are very territorial animals that mark and establish their domain with the scent of their own urine. Lions are the most social of the cat family. They live in family groups called *prides,* which consist of about fifteen lions. Typically, the pride's male would mark the *borders* of the group's territory by spraying surrounding vegetation with his pungent urine. Unwelcome animals would detect the strong scent and steer clear. The lion is a creature of dominion in the true sense of the word!

Like him, Christ has given you authority to mark your territory as a king in the earth. The enemy sees and must steer clear. You are a leader of the human "pride." You are elevated among men, to protect humanity. You have the power to take charge of your environment and prevent the enemy from invading the lives of those around you. You are a lion of God, and you have the power to keep evil away. The circumstances and trials of life must obey and submit to you. Not the other way around!

YOU ARE A DIGNITARY. YOU ARE NOT A DESTITUTE.

Binding His foal to the vine and His donkey's colt to the choice vine, He washes His garments in wine and His clothes in the blood of grapes. His eyes are darker and more sparkling than wine, and His teeth whiter than milk (verses 11-12).

These verses portray images of beauty and dignity. A lion is a very majestic beast that is regal, stately, and grand in his appearance. His luxurious mane *(found only in males)*; sleek, unspotted coat; and graceful walk all make the lion a very striking creature to behold. Indeed, for all his beauty and strength, the title "king of the beasts" suits the lion very well. Without question he is one of the most charismatic animals on earth.

In Christ, you have a very special form. In Him, you become conformed to the image and likeness of God Himself. You are beautiful. You are unique. You are fearfully and wonderfully made!

You are not an ordinary person. You are royalty. You are a VIP. You are seated in the ruling cabinet of the God of the whole universe. God has *enveloped* you with glory and honor. You have access to all that the earth has to offer. God has withheld nothing from your hand. He has given you unimaginable prosperity and power.

CHAPTER TWELVE

WHAT YOU MUST DO TO OCCUPY YOUR LION POSITION

Without question, your position as a lion reveals how powerfully and mightily you are positioned in Christ. You are enthroned in heavenly places so that as the lion, you may reign and exercise God's authority in the earth. However, you need to understand that these lion-like features will not come to you automatically. There are certain steps that you must take to develop into the kind of "lion" Christian that God has made you in Christ.

Now, there are three prominent characteristics that define the lion's supremacy above other beasts:

1. Its strength.

2. Its confidence.

3. Its courage.

If you want to be a lion Christian that walks in dominion, you must take time to diligently cultivate these virtues.

A LION IS STRONG.
The first unique trait of a lion is its strength.

> A lion which is strongest among beasts, and
> turneth not away for any.

PROVERBS 30:30

The lion has a remarkably powerful build. Its body is very muscular. It also has incredibly strong back legs that are designed for pouncing. With its front legs, it takes hold of and pins down its prey. It can run up to fifty miles per hour for short distances and leap for as high as thirty-six feet. The lion's amazing strength also enables it to devour and take on prey that is much larger than itself. With its powerful jaws, a lion can carry an animal up to twice its weight! No beast, no matter how mighty, can intimidate a lion. Lions are virtually indomitable!

The lion attains and sustains its incredible strength by its voracious diet. Lions are not just big animals; they have equally huge appetites. It has been said that a male lion can eat up to seventy-five pounds of food in one meal. Without question, food is very important to a lion. They prefer to eat big mammals such as zebras, buffalos, warthogs, large antelopes, and even giraffes. Only when large animals are not available do they resort to feeding on smaller animals. In the jungle, starvation, not other creatures, is a lion's greatest threat.

In the same way, to stay spiritually strong and empowered against the enemy, you must have an insatiable lion-like appetite for the Word of God, which is your spiritual food. When you feed and feast plentifully on God's Word, you will grow strong.

> …desire the pure milk of the word, that you may grow thereby.

> 1 PETER 2: 2

Moreover, just as the lion prefers to feed on large prey, you must not be satisfied to only feed on the "milk" of the Word alone. Your spiritual diet should not only consist of the *rudiments,* or basics, of the Word. Rather, you should have an ever-expanding spiritual diet that includes what the apostle Paul calls the "strong meat" of God's Word.

> For every one that useth milk is unskillful in the word of righteousness: for he is a babe. But strong meat belongeth to them that are of full age, even those who by reason of use have their senses exercised to discern both good and evil.

> *HEBREWS 5:14-15*

In infancy, milk is sufficient as a principal source of food. However, to develop and grow into a healthy and mature human being, a person must include solid foods in his or her diet.

You cannot develop into a strong Christian who terrorizes the devil unless you mature and continually feast on the strong meat of the Word. When you are spiritually strong, you will overcome the devil, the wicked one.

> I have written to you, young men, because you are strong, and the word of God abides in you, and you have overcome the wicked one.
>
> *1 JOHN 2:14B*

The Word of God is the source and sustainer of your spiritual strength. You must never stop increasing in your knowledge and understanding of God's Word. A huge diet empowers the lion and preserves its destiny as the "king of the jungle." Likewise, to reign in life and walk in dominion, you must voraciously feast upon God's Word. You cannot afford to *consume* His Word *scantily* or *sparsely*.

Do not be satisfied to be *fed* only when you come to church. Develop a habit of spending *quality* time on your own in the study of the Scriptures. This way you will never be defeated or ashamed in life.

> Study to shew thyself approved unto God, a workman that needeth not to be ashamed, rightly dividing the word of truth.
>
> *2 TIMOTHY 2:15*

The more you increase in your knowledge and understanding of God's Word, the stronger you will be spiritually. You will gain the strength that you need to confront and conquer every wile of the devil.

> The Word of God is the source and sustainer of your spiritual strength.

> A wise man is strong, Yes, a man of knowledge increases strength.

> PROVERBS 24:5

In contrast, without the wisdom and knowledge of God, you will be weak. You will lack the stamina to withstand the enemy's aggravations. Every problem in life can be traced to a lack of divine wisdom. A believer who has little or no knowledge of God's Word will very likely give in to defeat and frustration in life. Divine knowledge is what stabilizes you in the day of adversity.

> Wisdom and knowledge will be the stability of your times, and the strength of salvation; The fear of the LORD is His treasure.

> ISAIAH 33:6

Without the strength that comes from a consistent and profuse study of God's Word, a believer will most definitely fall prey to the devil in times of trial or temptation.

If you faint in the day of adversity, your strength is small.

PROVERBS 24:10

God wants you to stand and not fall in the "evil day." In your spiritual arsenal, He has included "the sword," which is the Word of God, so that you can overcome the enemy each time he comes against you.

Finally, my brethren, be strong in the Lord and in the power of His might. Put on the whole armor of God, that you may be able to stand against the wiles of the devil. ... Therefore take up the whole armor of God, that you may be able to withstand in the evil day, and having done all, to stand... And take the helmet of salvation, and the sword of the Spirit, which is the word of God.

EPHESIANS 6:10-11, 17

When you are equipped with the wisdom and knowledge of God's Word, you will surely stand firm in the midst of turbulence. You will never be moved by contrary situations. Remember: *Wisdom and knowledge will be the **stability** of your times, and the strength of salvation; The fear of the LORD is His treasure (Isaiah 33:6).*

Please understand that it is **your** responsibility to feast upon God's Word. The knowledge of the Word will not come to you automatically. God will not cut your brain open and surgically implant a *microchip* of the Bible into you. You must determine daily *(not once in a while)* to study God's Word for yourself.

It is important to state at this point that you should endeavor to have a "balanced diet" of the Word. Do not just concentrate on some areas and neglect others. Strive to grow and increase in your understanding of God's total Word.

Some believers know a lot about what God has to say concerning financial prosperity, but they have no clue as to what He has to say about righteousness and purity. Others know a lot about what the Word says concerning spiritual warfare, yet they know little or nothing about what He has to say about their health and physical wellbeing. There are still others who know what God has to say about the gifts and manifestations of the Spirit, yet they are ignorant about the leading and the fruit of the Spirit.

Where the battles of life are concerned, you are only as strong as your weakest point. If you are strong in your knowledge of what God's Word says concerning some areas of life, yet are ignorant or weak in others, you will not be as effective as you should be against the devil. So do not just focus on your *favorite* aspects of Scripture. Study the entire Word. Strive to be a well-balanced Christian!

> **Be well balanced** (temperate, sober of mind), be vigilant and cautious at all times; for that enemy of yours, the devil, roams around like a lion roaring [in fierce hunger], seeking someone to seize upon and devour. Withstand him; be firm in faith [against his onset—rooted, established, strong, immovable, and determined].
>
> 1 PETER 5:8-9A (AMP)

> For maximum victory and dominion in life study to know the whole counsel of God!

Seek to know and understand what God has to say about every aspect of your life—*for maximum victory and dominion in life study to know the whole counsel of God.*

For I never shrank or kept back or fell short from declaring to you **the whole purpose and plan and counsel of God.**

ACTS 20:27 (AMP)

A LION IS CONFIDENT

The second outstanding trait of a lion is his **confidence**. The lion is by no means a timid or shy creature. A lion is fully aware of his mighty strength and power. As a result, he does not walk carelessly. The lion moves and carries itself majestically. He is "...stately in walk."

He also exudes great confidence in his roar, which strikes terror in other animals.

> The fear of a king is as the **roaring of a lion**: whoso provoketh him to anger sinneth against his own soul.

PROVERBS 20:2

This is a sharp contrast to the way some believers carry themselves. When going through tough times, some go about looking dejected, sorry-faced, and sad. I have concluded that some believers look like they fear the devil more than God.

Beloved, no matter what you are going through, never walk with your head bowed down in despair. No matter the situation, square your shoulders, look up confidently, and say, "In Christ, I am a lion. I am a king and lord over this situation. It will not get the better of me. I will get the better of it! God and I are an unbeatable team."

It was with such confidence that David confronted Goliath. David was 100-percent sure of victory even before he felled the giant with the fatal stone. He addressed Goliath with great confidence and power:

> Then David said to the Philistine, "You come to me with a sword, with a spear, and with a javelin. But I come to you in the name of the LORD of hosts, the God of the armies of Israel, whom you have defied. This day the LORD will deliver you into my hand, and I will strike you and take your head from you. And this day I will give the carcasses of the camp of the Philistines to the birds of the air and the wild beasts of the earth, that all the earth may know that there is a God in Israel. Then all this assembly shall know that the LORD does not save with sword and spear; for the battle is the LORD's, and He will give you into our hands."
>
> 1 SAMUEL 17:45-47

It is interesting to note that David made all these bold declarations before he "physically" defeated Goliath. He despised Goliath's gigantic and towering frame because he was confident in the fact that the Lord His God who was with him was mightier than Goliath. He knew that though the giant was a tough opponent, with God's help, he would most assuredly defeat him. David knew, without a shadow of doubt, that he would not fall before his enemy.

> But the LORD is with me as a mighty, awesome One. Therefore my persecutors will stumble, and will not prevail. They will be greatly ashamed, for they will not prosper. Their everlasting confusion will never be forgotten.

> JEREMIAH 20:11

Beloved, under the new covenant, you have a better assurance than David did. Not only is your great God with you, He is in you! Jesus in you is greater than any *giant* that you may face.

> You are of God, little children, and have overcome them, because He who is in you is greater than He who is in the world.

> 1 JOHN 4:4

Sadly, many Christians are panic-stricken when faced with a challenging situation. They behave like timid *chickens* when confronted by the enemy. They completely forget that they have the backing of their great, omnipotent God. They are unsure or unaware of the strength and power that they possess in Christ.

Beloved, do not respond to a challenge with panic. Remember the saying: Why worry when you can pray? Worry does no good. It does not have the power to change your situation. It will only make things worse. This is because panic has a paralyzing effect on a person. A panic-stricken soldier, though powerfully armed, will become incapacitated in the presence of his enemy. In the battle-field, he will stay frozen and glued on one spot till the enemy comes and finishes him off.

There are many soldiers in Jesus' army today who tremble and are fearful in the presence of satanic opposition. The devil is quick to sense their panic, and he takes full advantage of them. He harasses their families, finances, marriage, career, and so forth, wreaking great pain and havoc in their lives. What a shame! How are the mighty fallen? This is such a sad irony. It is not your portion in Jesus' name.

In Christ you have the upper hand. Even a "day-old" believer is far more powerful than the devil. The devil is no match for you. In Christ, you are more than a conqueror.

> Yet in all these things we are more than conquer-ors through Him who loved us.
>
> ROMANS 8:37

Talk and walk like a conqueror. *Speak* with great confidence to every *towering mountain* that has intimidated you for so long. At your word, they will move. They will be cast into the sea.

> So Jesus answered and said to them, "Have faith in God. For assuredly, I say to you, whoever says to this mountain, 'Be removed and be cast into the sea,' and does not doubt in his heart, but believes that those things he says will be done,

he will have whatever he says. Therefore I say to you, whatever things you ask when you pray, believe that you receive them, and you will have them."

MARK 11:22-24

Remember, mountains are stationary objects. They will not move unless you move them. Do not be mistaken and think that your challenging situation will just fade away after some time. No! You must take action. God never told you to ignore the devil. He said to resist him strongly and confidently in faith (*1 Peter 5:8-9*). Make a bold confident move to confront every problem with the lion-like confidence that you have in Christ.

> Mountains are stationary objects. They will not move unless you move them!

No matter what situation you face in life, have the firm belief that you will triumph over it. It is impossible for any evil to dominate you because you are seated above in Christ. You are above every contrary circumstances. He who is above is above all (*John 3:31*).

The Lord made you a lion in the earth. Never ever doubt who you are in Him. Always be fully assured and confident of the power that you possess in Him. Let your talk be with a roar. Walk majestically, displaying unshakable confidence. Intimidate and terrorize the devil by your bold declaration of God's Word. The sight of a confident believer sends shivers down the devil's spine.

The story was once told of a great healing evangelist who was especially known for his remarkable confidence and boldness. It was even reported that his very presence sent demons fleeing!

There was one particular incident that occurred during one of his crusades. The meeting had just started when a demon-possessed man ascended the stage in a violent fit of rage. No one could restrain him. When the man of God was informed, he confidently approached the demoniac and, looking straight into his eyes, he said, "I am so and so." With confidence he introduced himself as a son of the Most High God. The demon immediately left the man, and he was instantly delivered.

Another account was given about a minister from Africa who through confidence in God thwarted a widely publicized witches' convention. The witches had appeared on the local TV station and announced their planned worldwide convention. They had arrogantly claimed that even if God came down from heaven their meeting could not be stopped.

In response, the man of God confidently said, "Well, God does not have to come down from heaven. His sons are in this town (*evidently referring to himself and believers like him*) and they are enough to foil your meeting." Needless to say, the witches' convention never took place. The devil's plan was stopped even before he had a chance to carry it out! This is the power of a confident believer.

Beloved, do not allow the adversities of life to trouble you any longer. Remain secure in your divine strength. We are children of the King of kings, and our shout must be the shout of a king. Like a lion's roar, the very sight of you should cast fear in the enemy's camp.

> The fear of a king is as the roaring of a lion…
>
> PROVERBS 20:2A

The enemy's threats should not intimidate you. You can make the devil flee in fear from your presence. Break his back-bone by your confident declaration of God's Word.

> For the word of a king is authority and power, and who can say to him, What are you doing?
>
> ECCLESIASTES 8:4

When you understand and are fully aware of the power that is yours in Christ, when you realize that in Him you are a lion, you will be full of confidence. You will mark your territory confidently. The enemy will see and steer clear. Should the devourer try to venture into your domain, it is he, not you, who will be the victim.

A LION IS BOLD

Last but not the least, another quality that is associated with a lion is the virtue of boldness.

> The wicked flee when no man pursueth: but the righteous are bold as a lion.
>
> PROVERBS 28:1

Boldness is confidence in action. A lion's strength empowers it. His confidence keeps him motivated. However, it is by his boldness that the lion actually executes or carries out his attacks. Through boldness and courage, it pounces upon and ultimately brings down its prey.

Without boldness, no matter how confident you are, like the proverbial dog you would just be "all bark and no bite." If you have confidence without boldness, your boast would be nothing more than an empty shout.

There are many Christians who are confident of the incredible power that they possess in Christ, yet they never make a move against the enemy in the face of attack. To truly experience victory and dominion in life, you must not just be confident. You must be brave and courageous. Boldness is confidence in action.

When I think of a bold believer, one of the people who instantly comes to mind is my mother-in-law. She is a woman who possesses courage that can only come from a rock solid confidence in God.

One evening in 1996, as she was driving into her yard, a gang of armed robbers ambushed her. Yet the sight of these fearful looking men did not trouble Mom. When their leader gruffly asked her and those with her to lay flat on the floor, she totally refused to comply. Squaring her shoulders and looking them straight in the eye, she boldly replied, "I will not lie down. God forbid that I should bow down to the devil!"

The robbers were shocked. They probably had never been confronted in such a way before. Baffled and confused by her boldness, they threatened to shoot her if she spoke like that again. But Mom could not be silenced. With greater courage she said, "In the name of Jesus not a single bullet will be shot in this house!"

I believe with all my heart that Mom won the battle right there and then. Her boldness must have gotten God's attention because He intervened in a supernatural way. All of a sudden, while the robbers were still searching the house for loot, they claimed to hear loud *noises* in the street. Disoriented and distracted, they rushed out of Mom's house as hastily as they had entered, never to return again. Glory to God!

No one in the house was harmed that day. On the contrary, the bandits left in shame and disgrace. I believe God wants us to be like Mom—bold and confident in the face of enemy attack. However such boldness does not come by accident. It comes by assurance of your covenant position in Christ. If you make such a boast without really knowing who you are in Christ, it may backfire. Such was the humiliating experience of the sons of Sceva.

> Then some of the itinerant Jewish exorcists took it upon themselves to call the name of the Lord Jesus over those who had evil spirits, saying, "We exorcise you by the Jesus whom Paul preaches." Also there were seven sons of Sceva, a Jewish chief priest, who did so. And the evil spirit answered and said, "Jesus I know, and Paul I know; but who are

you?" Then the man in whom the evil spirit was leaped on them, overpowered them, and prevailed against them, so that they fled out of that house naked and wounded.

ACTS 19:13-16

It is one thing for you to say with your mouth, "I am God's son," but it is another thing for you to really know deep in your heart that you are His. Confession without conviction is powerless. You can confess till you are blue in the face that you are a lion of God. But unless you are truly convinced in your heart, your confession will be empty and powerless.

Many have confessed till they became *confused*. They have tried to name and claim God's promises without truly believing the words that they

> Confession without conviction is powerless!

were confessing. A parrot can mimic words; yet the words really have no meaning to him. He is just repeating the words he hears from others. He does not have a personal revelation or insight into the power of the words that He utters. But when you confess with great conviction that you are a lion of God, you will stand confidently and victoriously against the enemy.

Every challenge of life is a wonderful opportunity to exercise your dominion authority over the devil. Yet you need to be bold to confront and engage him in battle. Without it you cannot be a man of dominion.

> When you confess with great conviction that you are a lion of God, you will stand confidently and victoriously against the enemy.

You also need boldness to possess all that God has given you in Christ. As Joshua was about to lead the Israelites to possess the Promised Land, God strongly admonished him to be bold.

Every place that the sole of your foot will tread upon I have given you, as I said to Moses ... **No man shall be able to stand before you all the days of your life**; as I was with Moses, so I will be with you. I will not leave you nor forsake you. **Be strong and of good courage**, for to this people you shall divide as an inheritance the land which I swore to their fathers to give them. Only **be strong and very courageous**, that you may observe to do according to all the law which Moses My servant commanded you; do not turn from it to the right hand or to the left, that you may prosper wherever you go ... Have I not commanded you? Be **strong and of good courage**; do not be afraid, nor be dismayed, for the LORD your God is with you wherever you go.

JOSHUA 1:3, 5-7

Without a lion's heart, you cannot enter into your Canaan land of promise. You need a heart of a lion to crush every opposition. Therefore, *for every confident confession of faith that you make, you must take a corresponding action of courage*. To conquer lands and walk in dominion, you must take bold steps of faith.

RIGHTEOUSNESS: THE KEY TO BOLDNESS

The wicked flee when no one pursues, but the righteous are bold as a lion.

PROVERBS 28:1

Basically, boldness is a product of righteousness. Without righteousness, you cannot exercise the boldness that you need to resist the devil. Before you make any attempt to take action against the enemy, you must first ascertain that you are standing uprightly and just before the Lord.

> For though we walk in the flesh, we do not war according to the flesh. For the weapons of our warfare are not carnal but mighty in God for pulling down strongholds, casting down arguments and every high thing that exalts itself against the knowledge of God, bringing every thought into captivity to the obedience of Christ, and being ready to punish all disobedience when your obedience is fulfilled.

> For every confident confession of faith that you make, you must take a corresponding action of courage.

2 CORINTHIANS 10:3-6

The simplest definition of righteous is: 100-percent FULL obedience to God. If your obedience to God is not FULL, you cannot stand against the enemy in battle. You cannot receive the breakthrough that you desire in life.

Sin makes a person weak, vulnerable, and exposed to the devil. To face the devil with sin is like a soldier who foolishly confronts his enemy with no armor on (Exodus 32:25). Unless you fully submit yourself to God's authority and lordship, you will not be in a position to resist the devil.

> Therefore submit to God. Resist the devil and he will flee from you. Draw near to God and He will draw near to you. Cleanse your hands, you sinners; and purify your hearts, you double-minded.

> JAMES 4:7-8

Moreover, if you regard iniquity in your heart, God will not hear you. If God does not hear you, how can you be helped? Without His mighty arm to help you in battle, how can you prevail against the enemy? To go into battle without the backing of God is catastrophic! This was what the Israelites discovered when, in their sinful and rebellious state, they chose to face their enemies in battle:

> But Moses said, Why now do you transgress the command of the LORD [to turn back by way of the Red Sea], since it will not succeed? Go not up, for the LORD is not among you, that you be not struck down before your enemies. For the Amalekites and the Canaanites are there before you, and you shall fall by the sword. Because you have turned away from following after the LORD, therefore the LORD will not be with you. But they presumed to go up to the

heights of the hill country; however, neither the ark of the covenant of the LORD nor Moses departed out of the camp. Then the Amalekites came down and the Canaanites who dwelt in that hill country and smote the Israelites and beat them back, even as far as Hormah.

NUMBERS 14:41-45

God encamps around the righteous. The righteous are bold because they can be sure of God's backing. When God is with you, you are unbeatable!

The eyes of the Lord are on the righteous, and His ears are open to their cry.

PSALM 34:15-17

Beloved, when you became saved you became the righteousness of God in Christ. However, to live a life of victory, you must steer clear from sin. If you indulge in a sinful lifestyle you will set yourself up for certain defeat. If you want to be bold and occupy your position as a lion of God, if you want to walk in dominion all the days of your life, you must be willing to make a lifetime commitment to righteous living.

Chapter Thirteen

You Are a Son

...the third living creature had a face like a man...

Revelation 4:7

In the vision that John the Revelator saw, you would notice that the face of the third creature around God's throne was that of a man. It was not a boy's face. This signifies that only grown men ascend thrones. Only matured sons can reign from the "throne" that God has prepared for them in the heavenlies.

In God's kingdom, there are **children** of God and there are **sons** of God. If you want to walk in dominion, it is extremely important for you not to remain a "baby Christian." You must mature into sonhood. Responsibility and rulership are entrusted into the hands of sons, *not* children.

> For unto us a Child is born, unto us a Son is given;
> And the government will be upon His shoulder.

ISAIAH 9:6

This prophecy concerning Jesus was not completely fulfilled in His life while He lay as a baby in the manger. NO! The government was placed upon Jesus' shoulders **after** He became a full-grown Son. It was not until Jesus grew into maturity that His earthly ministry found full expression.

> And the Child (Jesus) grew and became strong
> in spirit, filled with wisdom; and the grace of
> God was upon Him.

LUKE 2:40

Jesus grew and *became* a Son. Up to a certain point in His life, Jesus was referred to as a "child." But He did not remain a child forever. After He had grown, He was no longer called "Child"; He was called "Son."

Our Lord Jesus, God Incarnate Himself, had to grow up to sonship maturity before He could walk in the fullness of God's power in the earth. How much more will you? Beloved, until you grow up and become a son, you will not be able to experience dominion in life. You will not be able to fulfill your divine destiny.

It is only as a son that you can impact your world for Christ. God has ordained you to reign in life as a king and a priest. He has sent you to enforce His authority and will in the earth. However, you cannot accomplish this as a baby Christian. This is because your growth and maturity determines your level of competence. Every throne needs mature sons, not children.

> Woe to you, O land, when your king is a child, and your princes feast in the morning! Blessed are you, O land, when your king is the son of nobles, and your princes feast at the proper time—for strength and not for drunkenness!

ECCLESIASTES 10:16-17

Unless you mature into "sonhood," you cannot experience the dominion lifestyle that God has ordained for you. It is simply not possible for a babe or a child to walk in the fullness of his or her divine inheritance in Christ.

Bill Gates is purportedly the wealthiest man alive today. However, until they attain the age of maturity, none of his children would be able to lay claim to the vast inheritance which they have in him. Similarly, in Christ, you are an heir of God.

> And if you are Christ's, then you are Abraham's seed, and heirs according to the promise.

GALATIANS 3:29

> The level of your Christian growth will determine the extent of dominion authority that you will be able to exert.

God has given you everything that pertains to life and godliness (*1 Peter 1:3*). However, as Paul goes on to explain in the fourth chapter of Galatians, your ability to claim your great and unimaginable riches depends upon the level of your spiritual maturity. In order for you to receive all that God has for you, you must determine not to remain a child. You must grow up into sonhood.

> Now I say that the heir, as long as he is a child, does not differ at all from a slave, though he is master of all.

> GALATIANS 4:1

The Amplified Version states it more explicitly:

> *Now what I mean is that as long as the inheritor (heir) is a child and **under age**, he does not differ from a slave, although he is the master of all the estate.*

The implication of this is clear. Though you inherited and became master of your God-given estate, right from the time you became born again, you can only benefit from your vast divine inheritance as you grow up and mature.

Even in today's society, there are certain things that a grown person can do that a child cannot do. For instance, if you are underage, you cannot drive a car, get married, or vote. A person's performance in any area of life is directly related to his or her level of growth and development in that area. This is why in corporate America much emphasis is being laid on continuous training and personal development. Typically, employers give those whom they hire responsibilities and privileges that match their level of growth.

It is no different in the spiritual realm. The level of your Christian growth will determine the extent of dominion authority that you will be able to exert. It will also dictate the level of responsibility that God will commit into your hands.

You cannot afford to stop growing spiritually. Unless you develop from the level of babyhood and become a grown son of God, you simply cannot walk in dominion. If you are not a son, you cannot do any exploits for Him. It is only as a son that you can bring glory and honor to His name.

Children Are Born, but Sons Are Given!

> For unto us a **Child is born**, unto us a **Son** is given.
>
> *Isaiah 9:6a*

Now, you began your life here on earth as a baby. In the same way, on the day that you became born again, you were "born" into the kingdom of God, as a spiritual infant. However, it is not just enough for you to be born into the kingdom of God. You must also "grow on" and become a son!

Most Christians today are not fruitful because they are still *stuck* in the baby stage of their Christian lives. This is why their unbelieving friends, colleagues, loved ones, neighbors, and so forth do not feel their impact. Their "light" is not shining as Jesus said it should.

> Let your light so shine before men, that they may see your good works and glorify your Father in heaven.
>
> MATTHEW 5:16

Statistics reveal that Christianity is the fastest growing religion in the world. Since this is the case, the Church should make a greater impact than what currently exists. There are still countless numbers of unsaved people in the world today. It took only twelve men to turn the world upside down during the days of the early Christians. Why? They impacted their world for Christ because they *refused* to remain baby Christians. After their conversion, they matured to become sons who shook their world for Christ!

Most Christians today cannot even turn their own families upside down for Jesus, let alone the whole world! Sadly, only a very few among the countless number of self-professed believers are actually impacting lives for the Lord. This should not be so.

The world has seen many children of God. They have heard many people who claim to be Christians. But to be honest, they are tired of religious church folk whose lives do not reflect the power and glory of the risen Christ.

Now they are hungry for something different. They long for deliverers and saviors, people in whose hands lies the answer to their deepest needs. Yes! The world is eagerly waiting for the manifestation of God's sons.

> For the earnest expectation of the creation eagerly waits for the revealing of the sons of God.
>
> ROMANS 8:19

If you are wondering how you can let your light shine for Christ, all you need to do is to make a commitment to keep growing in your walk with God. It does not matter how long you have been a Christian. You need to keep on growing.

The more you grow spiritually, the more you will shine. You will do great exploits for the Lord your God. The unsaved around you will see and give glory to His name! It is high time for every believer on the surface of the earth to rise up and manifest his or her sonship authority. It is time for you to manifest your authority!

BASIC STAGES OF CHRISTIAN GROWTH

Growth is a process. According to the Bible, you and I are like *trees*, planted by God (*Isaiah 61:3b*). Just as it takes time for a seed to mature to the fruit-bearing stage, so also the sons of God are *grown* over a process of time. They do not emerge in an instant.

> And He (Jesus) said, "The kingdom of God is as if a man should scatter seed on the ground, and should sleep by night and rise by day, and the seed should sprout and grow, he himself

does not know how. For the earth yields crops by itself: first the blade, then the head, after that the full grain in the head. But when the grain ripens, immediately he puts in the sickle, because the harvest has come."

MARK 4:26-29

Trees do not grow overnight. Neither do believers! According to Jesus' parable, there are four basic stages of a plant's growth that are similar to a Christian's journey from infancy to sonhood.

1. The seed represents the infancy or newborn stage.

2. The blade represents the toddler stage.

3. The head represents the adulthood stage.

4. The full grain represents the fatherhood stage.

STAGE ONE: INFANT OR BABYHOOD STAGE

Every born-again Christian starts his or her spiritual journey as a seed that is planted by God. This was our position when we first came to the Lord. Every son of God, including our Lord Jesus, started at the birth stage—*"For unto us a Child is born...."*

Believe it or not, every great *giant* of the faith—your favorite man or woman of God—started his or her Christian experience as a tiny spiritual baby. As it is in the natural, the infancy stage begins at birth. It starts from the moment a person becomes born again. It is a time when the newborn believer is pampered and doted over. Both the convert and the person who led him to Christ bask in the excitement of his conversion.

Like a natural baby, a new convert cannot do much for himself. He relies heavily on the prayers and support of his spiritual "parent."

A baby Christian literally has to be spoon-fed the Word of God. He can only digest the simple basics, or the "milk" of Scripture.

> For everyone who partakes only of milk is unskilled in the word of righteousness, for he is a babe.
>
> HEBREWS 5:13

It is a stage in which he must be taught. A baby Christian can hardly instruct others or serve in leadership position. They can barely take care of themselves, let alone assume responsibility over others. This was why the apostle Paul strongly warned his protégé Timothy against ordaining novices, or those who had newly come to the faith, into positions of authority and power:

> A bishop then must be blameless ... **not a novice**, lest being puffed up with pride he fall into the same condemnation as the devil.
>
> 1 TIMOTHY 3:2A, 6

As wonderful as infancy is, it is just the beginning of life. It is not the end of it. After you become born again, God expects you to develop and grow up into maturity. Grow on, become a son!

> As newborn babes, desire the pure milk of the word, that you may grow thereby.
>
> *1 PETER 2:2*

It is not God's will for you to remain a baby Christian forever. He expects you to grow. He wants you to move on to perfection.

> Therefore, leaving the discussion of the elementary principles of Christ, let us go on to perfection, not laying again the foundation of repentance from dead works and of faith toward God.
>
> *HEBREWS 6:1*

STAGE TWO: TODDLER OR LITTLE CHILDREN STAGE

This is the "blade stage." At this stage in planting, the seeds have firmly taken root in the ground and now begin to show visible signs of development. The plant's sturdy stalk breaks through the barrier of the ground and green leafy blades begin to emerge from its sides.

Similarly, the "blade" or toddler stage of Christian growth is the formative stage when a believer starts learning to "walk" with God. It is the period of a Christian's early spiritual development.

Like toddlers in the natural world who sometimes stumble when they are just learning to walk, in this childish state, a believer's Christian walk may be somewhat unstable. It is typical for believers at this stage to be unsure about their salvation. "Little children" may talk and walk like Christians, but they still need to be reminded that their sins have been forgiven.

Such was my wife's experience during the early days of her conversion. She was so unsure of her salvation that she responded to altar calls at almost every fellowship meeting. In those days, she constantly needed to be reassured that she was saved.

At this stage a person's faith is shaky and unstable. A toddler Christian may have skyrocketing faith today, yet be down tomorrow. It is a time of the wavy or roller-coaster experience: hot for God today and cold tomorrow, depending on the circumstances.

It is also a stage when the believer is vulnerable and may be easily deceived if care is not taken. It is important that they are grounded in the truth of God's Word, as it is not uncommon for toddler Christians to be tossed about by fallacies or any kind of evil doctrine.

> That we should no longer be children, tossed to and fro and carried about with every wind of doctrine, by the trickery of men, in the cunning craftiness of deceitful plotting.
>
> *Ephesians 4:14*

Toddler Christians are easily beset by their old sinful habits. They have not learned to subdue their former fleshly passions by the power of the Holy Spirit.

> And I, brethren, could not speak to you as to spiritual people but as to carnal, as to babes in Christ. I fed you with milk and not with solid food; for until now you were not able to receive it, and even now you are still not able; for you are still carnal. For where there are envy, strife, and divisions among you, are you not carnal and behaving like mere men?
>
> 1 CORINTHIANS 3:1-3

Intense intercession must be made to establish them in the faith.

> My little children, for whom I labor in birth again until Christ is formed in you.
>
> GALATIANS 4:19

Toddlers also tend to be very self-centered. The typical toddler is a *taker* and not a *giver*. Have you noticed that a toddler's most favorite word is *mine*? As far as a toddler is concerned, the world revolves around him and his wants. They hardly like to share. They are not sensitive or responsive to the needs of others.

In this stage, most believers are just content that they are going to heaven when they die. They could care less if millions upon millions around them are on their way to hell. They are saved, and that is all that matters. When they come to church, they come to have their needs met. They do not come to minister to others. They come to receive their breakthrough. They are not bothered about the cares or concerns of others.

When you see a believer change churches as if he were changing clothes, such a Christian is most likely a toddler Christian. Toddler Christians *believe*, but they do not *belong*. They love to go hopping from one church to the other like a butterfly goes from flower to flower. When they feel a church is not meeting "their needs," when they feel that there is no more "sweet nectar" to suck, they move on to another place. They never for one moment feel that they have a responsibility to make any contribution or input to their church home. They are takers. They are not givers!

Sadly, many congregations have so many Christians who have refused to move beyond the toddler stage even after several years of becoming born again. I once heard a man of God, who unhappily remarked that only about 30 percent of the people who attend church are really committed Christians. How tragic! This means that the remaining 70 percent are at the very least unsaved or "overgrown" babies or toddlers at the most.

Beloved, God does not want you to remain a toddler. Put off your childish behaviors of the past. It is time to move on from the basics of salvation. Move up to greater heights of sanctification. It is not just enough for you to be blessed and receive success from the Lord. Move on and make a significant impact on others. Move on from toddlerhood to the next stage … adulthood!

STAGE THREE: ADULTHOOD STAGE

This is the "head" stage. It is the time of leadership in which a believer's God-given potential emerges. He starts to walk in the fullness of his divine authority and privileges, a time when he begins to experience the reality of being the head and not the tail, above and not beneath.

It is also the stage of divine encounter. A believer at this stage has not just heard of the Lord. He has seen Him. He has experienced Him. He has touched Him.

> That which was from the beginning, which we have heard, which we have seen with our eyes, which we have looked upon, and our hands have handled, concerning the Word of life.
>
> 1 John 1:1

At this point, you are not a *spectator* believer who waits passively and watches things happen. No! You are an active Christian who makes things happen. You practically jump at every opportunity to put your faith into action.

> Your experience is not that of the roller coaster that goes up and down. It is more like a rocket! You are "shooting" upward in the faith, with ever-increasing strength.

As a result, you have experienced God move mightily for you countless number of times. You have faced tests, put your faith into action, and you have a track record of testimonies to show for it. No one needs to convince you whether or not God is real. You know Whom you have believed. You know for sure that you serve the Living God!

Moreover, sin is no longer an issue to you. You are progressively *conforming* to the image of Christ. You are not *compromising*. You are more stable and your walk is steady. You are daily walking in the Spirit's power. The lusts of the flesh no longer appeal to you. You have learned to lay aside weights and besetting sins. You are pressing toward the onward goal. You know your left from right; and right from wrong.

> But solid food belongs to those who are of full age, that is, those who by reason of use have their senses exercised to discern both good and evil.
>
> HEBREWS 5:14

In this stage your feet are more grounded in the Lord. Your steps are consistent and sure. Your experience is not that of the roller coaster that goes up and down. It is more like a rocket. You are "shooting" upward in the faith, with ever-increasing strength. You are steadily growing from one level of glory to the other, soaring into new heights in God every day.

It is at this point that a believer sheds away the "baby fat" of his infant days. You have put aside the childish behaviors of your toddler years. You have now become a grown son!

When I was a child, I spoke as a child, I understood as a child, I thought as a child; but when I became a man, I put away **childish** things.

1 CORINTHIANS 13: 11

At this point in time, you will begin to walk in dominion in the full sense of the word. This is the place where you truly reign in life as a Christian. Now you no longer need to be spoon-fed. You know who you are in Christ. You fully understand the implications of your heavenly seat, and you are taking full advantage of your covenant rights.

A mature Christian is one who is grown and established in the faith. He is no longer tossed by every wind of doctrine. He only needs to be advised, encouraged, and admonished as the occasion demands. Nevertheless, as glorious as this stage is, there is yet a position that is higher than the adulthood stage where your dominion can become virtually unlimited.

STAGE FOUR: FATHERHOOD STAGE

A spiritual father is one who "births" and mentors others in the faith. Please note that the word *father* is a generic term that includes both men and women. At this stage, you are a legend and a powerful influence in the Body of Christ. Your duties in the church become that of a mentor, teacher, or coach.

But as for you, speak the things which are proper for sound doctrine: that the older men be sober, reverent, temperate, sound in faith, in love, in patience; the older women likewise, that they be reverent in behavior, not slanderers, not given to much wine, teachers of good things—that they admonish the young women to love their husbands, to love their children, to be discreet, chaste, homemakers, good, obedient to their own husbands, that the word of God may not be blasphemed.

TITUS 2:1-5

The fatherhood stage is the point of reproduction. When a seed matures to a full ear of corn, it contains many more seeds within itself. Likewise, the fatherhood stage is the "full-grain" stage, whereby not only have you become a mature son of God, but you also "breed" sons for God. You are not just a disciple; you are a discipler of men!

At this point, I also need to state that a believer does not need to be an ordained minister before he or she assumes the role of a father in the Body of Christ. A father is not known by his title; he is known by his good example.

> At this stage, not only are you a son of God; you also "breed" sons for God!

For you yourselves know how you ought to follow us, for we were not disorderly among you; nor did we eat anyone's bread free of charge, but worked with labor and toil night and day, that we might not be a burden to any of you, not be-

cause we do not have authority, but to make our-
selves an example of how you should follow us.

2 THESSALONIANS 3:7-9

A true father is one whose life is worthy of emulation.

For though you might have ten thousand in-
structors in Christ, yet you do not have many
fathers; for in Christ Jesus I have begotten you
through the gospel. Therefore I urge you, imi-
tate me.

1 CORINTHIANS 4:15-16

A father is not
known by his title;
he is known by his
good example.

Like the apostle Paul, one of
the greatest fathers of the faith,
in this stage you can boldly say
to other believers, *"Be ye follow-
ers of me, even as I also am of
Christ"* (1 Corinthians 11:1).

Fatherhood is the destiny of every believer. God has
raised each and every Christian to bear fruit for Him. The
responsibility of soul-winning and discipleship does not belong to "ordained" ministers alone. Everyone who has
received Christ free gift of salvation is *duty-bound* to impact others with the life changing Gospel of the Lord Jesus
Christ.

Now all things are of God, who has reconciled
us to Himself through Jesus Christ, and has
given us the ministry of reconciliation, that is,

that God was in Christ reconciling the world to Himself, not imputing their trespasses to them, and has committed to us the word of reconciliation. Now then, we are ambassadors for Christ.

2 Corinthians 5:18-20a

God has chosen all Christians to bear fruit. He has appointed all believers *(not just pastors, apostles, teachers, and so forth)* to be fathers. Jesus said, "You did not choose Me, but I chose you and appointed you that you should go and bear fruit, and that your fruit should remain, that whatever you ask the Father in My name He may give you." Jesus did not just choose some. He chose all!

The fatherhood or full-grain stage is the place where God wants you to be. No matter how great you feel your Christian experience is, if you have not gotten to the point at which you begin to birth and parent others spiritually, you are incomplete. Strive to make an impact on the lives of the unsaved. Aim to help establish younger believers in the faith. God has raised you to disciple disciples. It is not just enough for you to be a son of God. You must also breed sons for Him.

What Stage Are You At?

The time has come for you to make an honest assessment of yourself. Considering all four stages of Christian growth, how do you rate? Pause for a moment as you ponder the question: "What stage am I at in my Christian growth?" It is important that you first know your current level before you can truly progress forward.

If you are still in the infant or toddler stage, identify the "baby fat" that you must shed to move forward. What childish things are you willing to put aside so that you may grow on into sonhood?

And if you are in the adult stage, remember, God still has more in store. The ultimate stage is the "fatherhood stage," where your dominion is virtually unlimited. It is not just enough for you to be a disciple of the Lord. You must also disciple people for the Lord. *Mature sons must also breed sons for God.*

Do not just be content to serve God in your local church. Now is the time to go to the marketplace and harvest souls "raw" for God. Invade your workplace, your neighborhood, your family, and seek out the unsaved. Snatch them from the awful fires of hell. Devote your time and energy to helping baby and toddler Christians grow in the Lord.

Regardless of what your level of Christian growth is, the most important thing is that you never stop growing. As long as you are in the earth, the opportunity for growth will always exist. Move up from your present stage and press on toward the ultimate. Grow on, become a son! Remember, the level of your Christian growth will determine the extent of dominion authority which you will be able to exert. Only sons can reign from the *throne* that God has prepared for them in the heavenly places. Which will you be—a childish Christian or a mature son? The choice is yours!

CHAPTER FOURTEEN

GROWING FROM CHILDHOOD TO SONHOOD

But we all, with unveiled face, beholding as in a mirror the glory of the Lord, are being transformed into the same image from glory to glory, just as by the Spirit of the Lord.

2 CORINTHIANS 3:18

Your spiritual maturity has absolutely nothing to do with your physical age or the number of years that you have been a Christian. Many congregations around the world are full of spiritual babies who have been members for several years. Though they have been "born again" for quite a while, they are still spiritually immature.

How then does a Christian develop spiritually? Your spiritual growth largely depends on the level of encounter that you have with God. The more God reveals Himself to you, the more you will grow in Him. As you behold Him in the room of prayer and in His Word, you will be transformed. It is in His presence that you become changed…you grow from glory to glory by the power of His Spirit.

In this sense, unlike in the physical, our spiritual growth never stops. It is a continuous process. As long as you are on this earth, there will always be opportunity to grow in the Lord. The only time we will come into full maturity is when we see Him face to face.

> When I was a child, I spoke as a child, I understood as a child, I thought as a child; but when I became a man, I put away childish things. For now we see in a mirror, dimly, but then face to face. Now I know in part, but then I shall know just as I also am known.

1 CORINTHIANS 13:11-12

Beloved, please give growth a chance in your life. No one ever graduates from the school of the Spirit. No matter how glorious your walk with God is right now, it can be better.

> Give growth a chance in your life. No one ever graduates from the school of the Spirit!

Do not be content to *coast* perpetually on the same level of spirituality. Move on! God has greater things in store. And the more you grow in Him, the more capable you will be to walk in dominion. Here are some key things you must do to ensure you are constantly growing and developing as a Christian.

1. BE WILLING TO EMBRACE CHANGE.

You have heard the adage, "Change is growth, and growth is change!" If you are not ready to change, you will not experience growth. In the natural, a baby undergoes so many changes as he matures. For instance, he changes from drinking milk to solid foods; from sucking his bottle to eating with a spoon. It would be a serious cause of concern to an infant's mother if he did not make these progressions. Can you imagine how absurd it would be for a six- or ten-year-old child to still wear diapers or drink from a baby bottle?

> Change is not always convenient, but it is necessary.

Well, it is no different in the realm of the Spirit. There is a time when you must give up merely drinking the milk of God's Word. You must move on to "strong meat." You must not only rely on the pastor's messages alone to be fed. You must study God's Word for yourself.

> For every one that useth milk is unskilful in the word of righteousness: for he is a babe. But strong meat belongeth to them that are of full age, even those who by reason of use have their senses exercised to discern both good and evil.
>
> HEBREWS 5:13-14 (KJV)

Typically, most people do not like change. They prefer to stay in their comfort zone. Change is not always convenient, but it is necessary. You cannot keep doing the same thing and expect different results. If you want something you have never had, you must be willing to do something that you have never done. Stop now and ask yourself this question: What am I willing to do differently to move to the next level of glory?

2. CONFRONT YOUR "GIANTS."

No one ever gets promoted without facing some sort of test or exam. This principle is true in every facet of life. It is also true in the realm of the Spirit. Everything you know and have learned from God's Word will be tested. This is inevitable! According to our Lord Jesus, tribulation or persecution will most definitely arise **because of the Word** (Matthew 13:21).

Yet, from God's viewpoint, those same trials are the stepping-stones to your promotion. Without them, you would not be able to move on to the next level of glory. It is sad that so many believers give up too quickly in the face of opposition. What could have been a stepping-stone to their promotion ends up becoming a *tombstone* that buries their dreams and keeps them from progressing. This is because rather than stand firm in faith against their giants, some just throw up their hands in despair and turn their backs from the enemy.

Beloved, quitters never win, and winners never quit! God does not want you to flee from the enemy. He wants you to resist every giant of your life firm in faith. Why? Well, because He is with you as a Mighty Terrible One. With Him on your side, every opposition will be confounded.

You need your giants for promotion and spiritual growth. Challenges produce champions of faith. Every great man or woman of God in the world today has a story to tell. Without Goliath, David would not have become the mighty champion of Israel. Are you facing any giant today? Do not be discouraged. Whether it is a giant of financial difficulty, or a giant that is attacking your health, that *giant* in your life will give way, in Jesus' mighty name.

Challenges of life will mature you when you do not run away from them. From God's eternal perspective, the "giants" in your life are there to usher you into your next level of glory.

So do not try to dodge your giant. Do not procrastinate or choose to face up to him at a

> Challenges produce champions of faith.

later time. Instead, confront all the "Goliaths" of your life today. Then you will become a strong and mature Christian. If you run from your opposition, you will lose your position. But if you face them with God's help, you will triumph always. After tests come testimonies!

3. PRACTICE THE WORD.

How do you become good at something? How do you develop your skill? Through practice! Practice develops a person's capabilities. Practice produces growth. Practice makes perfect.

In the sports world, it is a known fact that the most successful contestant is not necessarily the most skillful. On the contrary, the world's most renowned athletes credit their triumphs largely to their ability to faithfully stick to a daily training regimen. Right from the time of the ancient Olympics, athletes have been known to train long and hard to be on top of their game. They consistently work out, exercise, and practice their game several hours a day in order to stay on top.

In the same way, if you want to grow spiritually, you must steadfastly practice faith-building disciplines. A very vital spiritual discipline is your ability to study and practice God's Word. Without fail, every single day of your life, you must determine to practice God's Word. Keep on hearing and acting upon the Scriptures. Take advantage of every opportunity to put God's Word to use. Maturity is not a product of age or academic attainment. It is a product of use.

> For everyone who partakes only of milk is unskilled in the word of righteousness, for he is a babe. But solid food belongs to those who are of full age, that is, those who **by reason of use have their senses exercised to discern both good and evil.**
>
> *HEBREWS 5:13-14*

Be consistent in your efforts to grow spiritually. You may make some mistakes at first, but keep trying nonetheless. Practice living by every word that proceeds from God's mouth. Keep trying to obey every precept and principle that you read in Scripture. Keep perfecting your holiness in the fear of the Lord.

> Therefore, having these promises, beloved, let us cleanse ourselves from all filthiness of the flesh and spirit, perfecting holiness in the fear of God.
>
> 2 Corinthians 7:1

You are largely responsible for your growth. It is up to you to "work out" your salvation with fear and trembling (Philippians 2:12). The more you "work out," the more your spiritual muscles will develop! The spiritual exercises that you are willing to do every day will ultimately determine the level of your growth.

4. ABIDE IN HIM.

You cannot develop into a mature son without staying in God's presence. If you desire to grow from childhood to sonhood, you must choose to daily "camp" with God in prayer and the study of His Word. He is the Source and Sustainer of your growth.

> Abide in Me, and I in you. As the branch cannot
> bear fruit of itself, unless it abides in the vine,
> neither can you, unless you abide in Me.
>
> JOHN 15:4

If you detach yourself from the Lord by ceasing to fellowship with Him, you will not grow. Ultimately such segregation will lead to death. It is only in Him that you have the capacity for growth. Your greatest responsibility as a believer is to keep your appointments with Him.

By *appointment* I am not just referring to your times of personal devotion. I am also referring to the times of corporate fellowship with other believers. They are just as important as your private times

> If you desire to grow from childhood to sonhood, you must choose to daily "camp" with God in prayer and the study of His Word.

with the Lord. Do not just go to church when you are in the mood or when you feel like it. Go always!

> Not forsaking the assembling of ourselves to-gether, as is the manner of some, but exhorting one another, and so much the more as you see the Day approaching.
>
> HEBREWS 10:25

When you fellowship corporately with others, you will be edified and built up. You will grow! Do not let your feelings determine when you will fellowship with God.

> Your greatest responsibility as a believer is to keep your appointments with Him.

As one of my precious sons in the ministry humorously says, "There are two times when you ought to come to church—when you feel like it and when you do not feel like it!" Even when you do not feel like praying, studying the Bible, or going to church, come before God regardless. Come just as you are. In His presence, your *apathy* will soon change to *affection*.

You simply cannot afford to be out of fellowship with God. It is in God's presence that you become changed. It was in the place of prayer that our Lord Jesus was transfigured. He was changed.

You therefore, beloved, since you know this beforehand, beware lest you also fall from your own steadfastness, being led away with the error of the wicked; but grow in the grace

> Do not abide in the world. Instead abide in the Word!

and knowledge of our Lord and Savior Jesus Christ. To Him be the glory both now and forever. Amen.

1 PETER 3:17-18

God's Word will mature you. The Bible is an amazing Book. You gain fresh insights each time you study God's Word. And the more you know, the more you will grow. So take His Word seriously.

Do not abide in the world. This will retard or stunt your Christian growth. Instead abide in the Word! There you will become transformed into Christ's image. You will grow into perfection in Christ.

And do not be conformed to this world, but be transformed by the renewing of your mind, that you may prove what is that good and acceptable and perfect will of God.

ROMANS 12:2

When you were a babe in Christ, the milk of the Word sustained you. But beyond that, the strong meat of the Word will produce life-transforming revelations that will "grow" you into a son. Remember: Growth is not a function of chronological age. It is a function of your encounter with God. The more God reveals Himself to you in the room of prayer and study of His Word, the more you will grow spiritually.

Only grown men ascend thrones. If you want to occupy your heavenly throne and walk in dominion in the earth, you must keep on maturing spiritually. Do not remain a child forever. Grow up. Become a son!

CHAPTER FIFTEEN
YOU ARE AN EAGLE

…the fourth living creature was like a flying eagle.

In the family of winged creatures, the eagle is definitely the king of the sky. The eagle is to the birds of the air what the lion is to the beasts of the field. Its ability to soar amazing heights in the fiercest of winds places the eagle in a class all by itself.

Eagles can fly higher and faster than other birds. They can actually soar at speeds of thirty miles per hour and dive at speeds of 100 miles per hour! No other bird on earth can rival the might and majesty of the incredible eagle.

There are three things which are **too wonderful** for me, Yes, four which I do not understand: **The way of an eagle in the air…**

PROVERBS 30:18-19A

For this reason, throughout the world the eagle has long been accepted as a symbol of valor, boldness, majesty, mobility, and invincibility. Many nations in the ancient world—the Greeks, Egyptians, and Romans among others—used the eagle as their national symbol. Specifically, the early Romans used the eagle's emblem on their shields of battle because it was the recognized symbol of the indomitable Roman Empire.

In our modern age, the national symbol for the greatest nation on the earth, the United States of America, is the American bald eagle with a spring of olive branches clutched in its right talon and a band of arrows in its left. So enormous is the significance of the eagle that the Almighty God, in reference to His people Israel, describes Himself as an eagle.

> You have seen what I did to the Egyptians, and how I bore you on eagles' wings and brought you to Myself.

> *EXODUS 19:4*

Here, God personally endorses or testifies to the strength, power, and importance of the eagle.

THE EAGLE AS A SYMBOL OF YOUR DOMINION

In Bible lands, two types of eagles are particularly significant—the Golden Eagle and the Imperial Eagle. This is because both species rightly represent two key aspects of who we are in Christ. The Golden Eagle likens us to being partakers of God's divine nature while the Imperial Eagle speaks of us as kings.

As partakers of His divine nature, we are God's sons. We have been called out of sin into holiness—out of darkness into God's marvelous light.

> But you are a chosen generation, a royal priesthood, a holy nation, His own special people, that you may proclaim the praises of Him who called you out of darkness into His marvelous light.

> 1 PETER 2:9

Unlike some other birds, such as the bat and the owl, the eagle is not a night bird. As a matter of fact, the eagle's eyesight is poorest at night. On the contrary, an eagle performs all his activities during daylight. Well, just as the eagle is a creature of light, so also are you a son of light. You belong to Jesus, who is the Light of the world.

> You are all sons of light and sons of the day. We are not of the night nor of darkness.

> 1 THESSALONIANS 5:5

Just as an eagle hunts, feeds, and flies in the light, so also God wants you to perform all your activities in the light of His Word. He does not want you to walk in the dark ways of the world. In Christ, you are an eagle and you are to walk in the light as He is in the light.

> This is the message which we have heard from Him and declare to you, that God is light and in Him is no darkness at all. If we say that we

have fellowship with Him, and walk in darkness, we lie and do not practice the truth. But if we walk in the light as He is in the light, we have fellowship with one another, and the blood of Jesus Christ His Son cleanses us from all sin.

1 JOHN 1:5-7

Cleanliness is one of the eagle's topmost priorities. The eagle is a very clean bird that spends a great part of his day cleaning. The mother eagle, for instance, constantly works hard to keep her nest clean, ridding it of debris and dirt. The eagle may also add fresh vegetation to the nest to cover up old food. Sometimes, an eagle may even move out of an old dirty nest for about a year or two. In this instance, he would build another nest nearby till the old nest is naturally cleaned out by the elements (i.e., rain, wind, etc). An eagle typically cannot stand a filthy environment!

As an eagle of God, you have also been called to live an impeccably "clean" lifestyle. You have been called out of darkness so that you may shine as His light in the midst of a crooked and perverse generation.

Do all things without complaining and disputing, that you may become blameless and harmless, children of God without fault in the midst of a crooked and perverse generation, among whom you shine as lights in the world.

PHILIPPIANS 2:14-15

It is abnormal for a person who claims to be saved and redeemed to continue to indulge in a sinful lifestyle. How can you say that you are redeemed from sin's power, and yet keep on sinning willfully? It is a sheer contradiction of terms. Contrary to what some people wrongly believe, grace is not a license to sin. It is your license to live above sin. It is the power that enables you to stay clean and live in holiness before the Lord.

> For sin shall not have dominion over you, for you are not under law but under grace. What then? Shall we sin because we are not under law but under grace? Certainly not!
>
> ROMANS 6:14-15

If you know and believe that Jesus is your Savior and Lord, then you must understand that you have the power to overcome every temptation. Yes! It is possible for you to live a life that is free and clean from the filth of sin. God has given you dominion over sin. Clean and righteous living is not an option for you. It is your obligation as a follower of Christ. Understand that you have been saved by grace. You are no longer a slave of sin. You are not a sinner. You are now a saint. Walk like a saint. Do not continue in your old sinful ways.

> Grace is not a license to sin. It is your license to live above sin!

> Therefore be imitators of God as dear children. But fornication and all uncleanness or covetousness, let it not even be named among you, as is fitting for saints; neither filthiness, nor foolish

talking, nor coarse jesting, which are not fitting, but rather giving of thanks. For this you know, that no fornicator, unclean person, nor covetous man, who is an idolater, has any inheritance in the kingdom of Christ and God.

EPHESIANS 5:1, 3-5

You and sin are no longer in the same class! You are seated in Christ, far above the evil defilement of sin. God's grace abounds from His throne unto you (Hebrews 4:14-16). His grace is your dominion authority over sin. Are you struggling with one bad habit after another? Is there a particular sin that always seems to make you fall? Whenever you feel this way, remember your position. Get your covenant bearing right—remember that you are an eagle. Sin is not above you. *You are above sin.*

Beloved, you do not have to fall to temptation. You are not weak. You are an eagle of God. You are seated in the heavenly realm. You are above sin. Like the eagle, give top priority to staying clean and unsoiled by sin. Make a firm commitment to righteousness because God has given you dominion over sin. Remember: You are no longer a sinner. You are no longer a slave to sin. You are no longer in darkness. No! You are a saint. You have dominion over sin. You are an eagle of God. You are a child of the Light. Walk and live like the saint that you are!

For you were once darkness, but now you are light in the Lord. Walk as children of light (for the fruit of the Spirit is in all goodness, righteousness, and truth), finding out what is

acceptable to the Lord. And have no fellowship
with the unfruitful works of darkness, but rather
expose them.

Ephesians 5:7-11

Not only do eagles steer clear from darkness, but
they also stay away from creatures of darkness. For
instance, one of the eagle's deadliest enemies is the
owl, a notorious creature of the night. In a similar
sense, as an eagle Christian, you are to steer clear from
every evil association.

Do not be unequally yoked together with unbelievers. For what fellowship has righteousness
with lawlessness? And what communion has
light with darkness?

2 Corinthians 6:14

As a son of the living God, you should have no dealings
with anything that pertains to darkness. Avoid bad company, bad places, and shady deals. You are a person of the
Light. You are an eagle of God!

Secondly, the imperial eagle symbolizes the kingly authority and power that Christians have in Christ.
Just as the eagle reigns supreme in the sky, afraid of
neither man, beast, nor the elements, in Christ you are
also a king. You are destined to reign. You were born
to dominate.

In the next chapter, we will examine the unique traits that make the eagle exalted among all birds. From our analysis of the eagle, you will observe how and why he reigns so powerfully in the sky. As you study the eagle's ways and observe his form, you will gain fresh insight into the position of power and kingly authority that you, too, have in Christ.

Chapter Sixteen
Why the Eagle
Is King of the Sky

Like the lion, its counterpart of the field, the eagle's majesty has a lot to do with its incredible build and unique personality. The eagle is one of the world's largest predatory birds. An eagle can weigh as much as fourteen pounds and measure as long as forty-two inches with wingspans stretching up to eight feet!

Just as the eagle possesses a distinct form, so also are you different from ordinary men. You are "fearfully and wonderfully made" (Psalm 139:14). As an eagle of God, you are *built* in an extraordinary and peculiar way because you were born to reign.

> And have made us kings and priests to our God;
> And we shall reign on the earth.

> REVELATION 5:10

Now let us examine these amazing characteristics that you, as a believer, have in common with the eagle. It is these traits that have helped the eagle earn his prized and coveted title—"king of the sky."

THE EAGLE IS A HIGH-FLYER.

Eagles typically venture into territories where other birds dare not fly. No other winged creature can soar as high as the eagle does. None even comes close to ascending to great breathtaking altitudes like the eagle. An eagle will sometimes soar to heights of more than 10,000 feet. They can fly at speeds of thirty miles per hour and dive for prey at speeds of 100 miles per hour.

Obviously, for this reason you will hardly find an eagle's nest on low planes. Instead, they build their nests on high trees and mountains. The eagle likes high places because he hates whatever is mediocre or common. He loves to soar far above average levels and stand distinct and supreme over all birds.

Now, in the human *race* of life, there are crawlers, there are walkers, there are runners, and there are flyers. The first three—the crawler, walker, and runner—all have to do with the earthly realm. They are constrained in two respects: They are limited both to and by the earth.

On the other hand, the flyers are not earthbound. They are heaven-bound. Nothing on earth can stop a flyer. He keeps soaring above the things that limit others. He aims high even beyond the skies.

Like the eagle, God has **designed** and **destined** you to be a **"high-flyer"** in life's journey. You are not a crawler, walker, or runner. It is not God's will for you to be stagnant or grounded in life. He wants you to keep soaring far above ground levels, rising high above the things that frustrate others. Through dominion, He has given you a superior mentality and ability to rise above every challenge of life.

Did you notice that the eagle that John described in Revelation 5 was *a flying* eagle? It was not a stationary or *grounded* eagle. This shows that as an eagle of God, it is an abomination for you to be grounded in life. It is an error!

Like the eagle, God built you to be a flyer. You are destined to keep going higher and higher in the race of life—moving from one level of glory to another. It is God's plan for you to keep aiming high—be above only, and never beneath.

Friend, are you weighed down by burdens and concerns? Are you overwhelmed by the pressures of this world? Allow the revelation of who you are thrust you

> God has **designed** and **destined** you to be a **"high-flyer"** in the race of life.

out of your present despair. Rise up strong in faith. Refuse to accept defeat or failure—you are an eagle of God. Amen!

You do not belong in the valley. You belong on the mountaintop. God has placed you far above all the things that typically limit or hinder others. He destined you to ride on the high places of the earth.

> As an eagle stirs up its nest, hovers over its young, spreading out its wings, taking them up, carrying them on its wings, so the LORD alone led him, and there was no foreign god with him. **"He made him ride in the heights of the earth**, that he might eat the produce of the fields; He made him draw honey from the rock, and oil from the flinty rock; Curds from the cattle, and milk of the flock, with fat of lambs; And rams of the breed of Bashan, and goats, with the choicest wheat; And you drank wine, the blood of the grapes."

DEUTERONOMY *32:11-14*

It is only in high places that an eagle can realize its full potential. On the ground the eagle is useless, unfulfilled, and unproductive. This is because like you, God has *designed* and destined the eagle to ride on high places. He was never meant to stay on the ground like other birds such as the chicken, turkey, peacock, and so forth.

As the eagle soars high above *ordinary* bird levels, he loses sight of the things that limits or troubles other creatures. This is because the higher the eagle soars, the more it can observe and avoid danger afar off. This is a privilege that is quite unique to the eagle.

The eagle has two sets of eyelids. One is used while the bird is stationed on the earth. The other protects the eagle when it is airborne from onrushing air and also against trees, bulrushes, or enemies. The eagle's second pair of eyes, coupled with his ability to fly high, enables him to rise above every turmoil and confusion, and glide into the realm of peace.

Please understand that God has placed incredible potential in you. He has *made you to ride in the heights of the earth*. You are not created for the low places. So do not limit yourself. Do not settle for anything less than the very best. Do not go for common grounds. Go for the choicest places. Prepare to move out of your comfort zone and aim high.

You will not realize what God can do in and through you until you embrace the eagle's mentality of superior living. You can only maximize your God-given potential when you chose to aim high. You cannot accomplish anything if you remain on an average or mediocre level.

In this sense, do not dream small dreams. Dream big! You are an eagle. Nothing on earth has the power to limit you in the pursuit of your God-given purpose. Not finances, not your skin color, not your background, not human bureaucracies ... NOTHING!

Typically, God will always give you a vision or dream that is bigger than you. This is because He created you for greatness. He made you to ride on high places. So put aside all the reasons why you think your dream cannot be achieved. Remember, nothing on earth can limit God, who sits high in the heavens. He that is above is above all! You belong to Him, so nothing can limit you either. Like an eagle, rise above the earthly realm, step out in faith, and do what God is calling you to do.

The Dominion International Center Testimony

Giving all glory and honor to God, I owe a great deal of my success in life and ministry to my understanding that in Christ I am an eagle. I have never let my present circumstances determine my obedience to God. I have learned to take great strides of faith when it seemed in the natural that all odds were against me. I am glad to say that God has never disappointed me. He is no respecter of persons, so I know that He will never disappoint you either!

> Nothing can stop you from getting what God has given!

One afternoon, in the year 2000, as I was driving into Houston, Texas, on my way from Dallas, the Holy Spirit spoke so clearly to me, *"It is time to purchase land for the church."* He then led me to an 18.3 acreage and said, *"Get that land now! I have reserved it for you."* Now, in the natural, this seemed to be an impossible order to follow. I reasoned within myself, *How old is the church that we should think of buying a piece of land now? We are not yet two years old. Where on earth are we going to get the resources to purchase such a vast place?*

However, over the years, I had learned never to limit God. He has taught me to aim high because in Him I am above all. I knew that since God had truly given us the land, nothing on earth could stop us from getting it. **Nothing can stop you from getting what God has given.** Absolutely nothing!

With this eagle mindset, right there in my car I made phone calls to my associate ministers at the time. They responded immediately and soon after joined me on the land. We promptly called the seller. And in a matter of moments, we began the process of negotiating the purchase of the land.

God gave us incredible favor with all the agencies involved, and one by one every *hurdle* was victoriously surmounted. To cut a long story short, about eleven months later, we became the grateful owners of a vast land. All this because I chose to operate as the eagle, which God has made me to be. I lost sight of the mundane and ordinary. I set my face on high and aligned myself with my great big God.

Today, the Dominion International Center campus stands majestically and magnificently on the land that God gave us, as a trophy of God's faithfulness and the eagle-like mentality that we possess in Christ. Though we faced great hurdles, we did not let them limit or keep us from realizing our God-given vision. To God be all the glory!

When you learn how to fly high, you will leave the realm of the ordinary into the extraordinary; the common to the uncommon; and the lowlands to the high lands. There is a geographical law that states that "the higher you go, the cooler it becomes." The higher you soar by the power and the current of the Holy Spirit, the cooler, or better, your life will be. You will not struggle like others do. You will soar and enjoy divine acceleration and promotion in all that you do. You will not be a *crawler*, *walker*, or *runner* in the race of life. You will be a *flyer*.

THE EAGLE IS STRONG, COURAGEOUS, AND RESILIENT.

The eagle is an extremely strong bird. An eagle can swoop down from the sky, pick up an animal off the ground that weighs as much as or more than it does, and then fly off with that animal in its talons.

In Christ, you are also incredibly strong and you can do all things. The words *can't* and *impossible* may affect others. But they do not apply to you. So do not shy away from challenges. Take them on! You have tremendous ability to accomplish great things. In Him you can literally do *all* things. There is absolutely no limit to the dominion power that is available to you in Christ Jesus.

> Now to Him who is able to do exceedingly abundantly above all that we ask or think, according to the power that works in us.
>
> *EPHESIANS 3:20*

Not only is the eagle strong in might, but he is also strong in mind! The eagle is a very resilient creature that never gives up. Nothing can shake an eagle's will to excel. There comes a time in the life of an eagle when he is slower in flight. His talons and beak become blunt. Yet he does not retire. On the contrary he *refires*.

He retreats, for a while, to a solitary place where he sheds his old feathers and talons. As new feathers and talons grow, his strength is renewed. He then comes back full of vitality and ready to keep on soaring and rising as the king of the sky.

One of the most amazing company comebacks in U.S corporate history is the IBM turnaround of the 1990s. In 1993, IBM was in a serious financial pit. That year, the company had posted an $8 billion loss. In addition to this, at the stock exchange, IBM shares, which had sold for $43 in 1987, had now plummeted to a miserably low $12.

There seemed to be no future for the computer company that had once ruled the world. Topnotch economists, in their financial reviews, had nothing but predictions of disaster and possible bankruptcy for the once-thriving technological giant. According to them, there was no way that IBM could make it among tough competitors like Microsoft who had now arrived on the scene.

But to the amazement of all the "prophets" of doom, IBM did not retire; it refired! It made its way out of the pit. That same year the wind of change blew into IBM when a man by the name of Lou Gerstner became its CEO. Lou, a former IBM customer, introduced a number of radical and innovative measures that helped transform the dying company back to prominence. So great was the turnaround, that by the beginning of the twenty-first century, IBM recorded profits to the tune of $8 billion. Imagine that! In less than a decade, IBM had gained back all that it had lost. Talk about a comeback.

Beloved, does it seem as if you are in a pit? Do you feel that you have recorded great loss in certain areas of your life? Perhaps, like IBM, you have found yourself in the pit of financial despair. Or it may be the pit of a terrifying disease, troubled marriage, depression, and so forth. Whatever troubling pit you have found yourself in, I am glad to tell you, you can come out of it! You are an eagle of God. You do not belong to the valley. You belong to the mountain. You belong to the high places of the earth.

Like IBM, you can recover every single thing that you have lost. God wants to bring you out of the pit and restore to you all the years that you have suffered loss. He wants to give you double for all your trouble.

> As for you also, **because of the blood of your covenant, I will set your prisoners free from the waterless pit.** Return to the stronghold, you prisoners of hope. **Even today I declare that I will restore double to you.**
>
> ZECHARIAH 9:11-12

> The words *can't* and *impossible* may affect others. But they do not apply to you!

But to experience your desired comeback, you must embrace the resilience of an eagle. You must refuse to accept the pit as your *fate*. You must determine, against all odds, to rise up out of it strong in *faith*. One of the key secrets to Lou's successful IBM turnaround was his winning attitude. He refused to give up in the face of hopelessness. He set a goal for winning, and he did not let anything stop him in his pursuit of it. He turned a deaf ear to all the negative voices of the financial "experts." He chose to maintain strong faith in IBM's bright future.

At times when you feel dry, stale, depressed, weak, or defeated, please remember that in Christ, you are an eagle. You must not give up in despair because it is not over until God says it is over.

Choose to follow the example of the eagle. Separate yourself unto the Lord. Take a few days off from the hustle and bustle of life. Wait upon God in prayer. Totally immerse yourself in His Word.

> Have you not known? Have you not heard? The everlasting God, the LORD, the Creator of the ends of the earth, neither faints nor is weary. His understanding is unsearchable. He gives power to the weak, and to those who have no might He increases strength. Even the youths shall faint and be weary, and the young men shall utterly fall, but those who wait on the LORD shall renew their strength; **They shall mount up with wings like eagles, they shall run and not be weary, they shall walk and not faint.**
>
> ISAIAH 40:28-31

In His presence you will shed your old *feathers*. You will change your weakness for God's strength. Ultimately, you will be refreshed, strengthened, and renewed, fully prepared to tackle and triumph over anything that comes your way.

Bless the LORD, O my soul; And all that is within me, bless His holy name! Bless the LORD, O my soul, and forget not all His benefits: Who forgives all your iniquities, who heals all your diseases, who redeems your life from destruction, **who crowns you with lovingkindness and tender mercies, who satisfies your mouth with good things, so that your youth is renewed like the eagle's.**

PSALM 103:1-5

Once you understand and accept the fact that you are an eagle, you will never again experience *burnout* in your walk with God. Instead, you will feel a never-ending *boost* of divine energy in your spiritual life. You will never lack the passion or power to serve God. Even in old age, you will still be fruitful and well able to accomplish God's purpose in the earth.

This was the testimony of Caleb, the great servant of God, who at the ripe old age of 85 was still strong enough to possess more of the land that he had inherited according to the promise of God. In his old age, Caleb was not an invalid. On the contrary, he was a pillar of strength. He was still able and willing to take on mountains for God.

"And now, behold, the LORD has kept me alive, as He said, these forty-five years, ever since the LORD spoke this word to Moses while Israel wandered in the wilderness; and now, here I am this day, eighty-five years old. As yet I am as strong this day as on the day that Moses sent me; just as my strength was then, so now is my strength for war, both for going out and for coming in. Now therefore, give me this mountain of which the LORD spoke in that day; for you heard in that day how the Anakim were there, and that the cities were great and fortified. It may be that the LORD will be with me, and I shall be able to drive them out as the LORD said." And Joshua blessed him, and gave Hebron to Caleb the son of Jephunneh as an inheritance.

JOSHUA 14:10-13

If Caleb, under the old covenant, could still possess lands and conquer mountains at the grand old age of eighty-five, how much more will you? Under the new covenant, the power of God does not just rest on you. It *resides* in you *(Ephesians 3:20)*. In this regard you are at a far greater advantage than Caleb or all the saints of old.

Beloved, it is possible for you to live *long* and *strong.* So do not picture yourself confined to a rocking chair in your old age. Do not imagine yourself ever running out of strength. You are an eagle. Even in old age, you will still be vibrant and active for the Lord. You will keep bearing fruit.

Those who are planted in the house of the LORD shall flourish in the courts of our God. They shall still bear fruit in old age; They shall be fresh and flourishing.

PSALM 92:13-14

Recently I heard of a group of eighty-year-old women who meet regularly to intercede and pray in England. These are eagle Christians in the fullest sense of the word. At eighty, they are not tired or retired. Instead, they are full of power and might, doing exploits for God on their knees.

> If you want a comeback, you must not give up!

Once you grasp the fact that you are an eagle of God, you will know that you are an incredibly powerful human being who can keep going strong, never once running out of strength. Your life will be a testimony of results. Your path will shine brighter and brighter. You will go from strength to strength and from glory to glory.

As an eagle of God, you must not give up in the face of a seemingly hopeless situation. Believe in the God of restoration. He will give you a fresh vision and new hope. He will give you strength to go on till you recover all that you had lost and more. *If you want a comeback, you must not give up.* Quitters never win and winners never quit. Winners subdue every opposition. Winners walk in dominion!

THE EAGLE HAS AMAZING VISION

The eagle has long been renowned to have extremely keen eyesight. An eagle's vision is about eight times sharper than a human's! It has been said that an eagle can spot stationary prey close to a mile away. This is why people who have an outstanding sense of vision are said to be "eagle-eyed."

The eagle owes its excellent vision to the fact that it has two areas of extra-acute vision that enable it to have both sideways and binocular vision. Imagine this: An eagle's scope of vision is 275 degrees. As the eagle flies in the sky, its eyes operate independently, allowing the bird to scan vast areas.

As an eagle Christian you also have two areas of acute vision—natural eyes for earthly vision and spiritual eyes for supernatural vision. It is a shame that in life's journey, some Christians only use their earthly vision. As a result, they are myopic and limited in their perception of life.

> While we do not look at the things which are seen, but at the things which are not seen. For the things which are seen are temporary, but the things which are not seen are eternal.
>
> 2 CORINTHIANS 4:18

The eagle is successful because he maximizes both areas of his vision. If you want to soar high in life, you must also engage your supernatural vision. Please understand that there is a limit to where your natural eyes can take you. If you view the world only through your natural vision, you will not go very far in life. You will live just for the temporal and give no regard to the things of eternal value.

Without spiritual vision, you can neither understand nor walk in the fullness of God's great purpose for your life. This is because the things of God cannot be perceived or received by the natural mind. It is only with the eyes of your spirit that you can grasp and gain all things that God has in store for you.

> But the natural man does not receive the things of the Spirit of God, for they are foolishness to him; nor can he know them, because they are spiritually discerned.
>
> *1 CORINTHIANS 2:14*

The reason why many people are not making any headway in their lives is because they cannot *see* God's divine plan for their lives. They have no clue as to what He has created them to do in the earth. They lack spiritual vision. Many dear saints have died without ever accomplishing their destinies because they lacked divine vision.

> Where there is no **vision**, the people perish.
>
> *PROVERBS 29:18A* (KJV)

If you want to attain great success in life, you must be a visionary. The greatest movers and shakers of our world—its leaders, philanthropists, inventors, scientists, educators, activists, social workers, writers, artists, and so forth—all have one thing in common. They were and are all visionaries.

Orville and Wilbur Wright, American inventors and aviation pioneers, saw the possibility of powered flight when others thought it was impossible. Their ability to see beyond the ordinary produced history's first powered, sustained, and controlled airplane, which rose from level ground without any assistance at take off.

Thomas Edison, who is by far one of the most accomplished inventors in the history of technology, was a great visionary. His inspiration for one of his most prominent inventions, the incandescent electric lamp, came during an exhibition where a series of eight glaring 500-candlepower arc lights where displayed. Others who attended the exhibition were probably excited and thrilled at this impressive sight. But not Edison! He envisioned something even greater. He saw beyond the ordinary and had a dream to create a safer and more efficient form of lighting.

In an age where lamps and candles were the only source of illumination, Thomas Edison, because of his ability to see beyond the ordinary, went on to invent a safe, mild, and inexpensive electric light that eventually replaced the gaslight and candlelight in millions of homes.

It is impossible to make your mark in the world if you are not a visionary. *When you see beyond what the average man sees, you will get more than what the average man has.* What's more, your chance of outstanding success in life is 100-percent guaranteed when you are a God-appointed visionary.

God will do nothing in your life until He has first **showed** you His plan. God simply cannot take you to a place that you cannot *see*. Amos 3:7 says, *"Surely the* LORD *God does nothing, unless He reveals His secret to His servants the proph-*

ets." And you can only *see* His plans through your spiritual eyes. We see this principle at work in the life of Abraham, the great father of faith.

> And the LORD said to Abram, after Lot had separated from him: "Lift your eyes now and look from the place where you are—northward, southward, eastward, and westward; for all the land which you see I give to you and your descendants forever."

GENESIS 13:14-15

Notice that God had a great plan to give Abraham a vast land and make him the father of many nations. Yet, the condition was that "all the land **which you see I give**…" In short, God told Abraham, "If you can see it, you will get it."

> God will do nothing in your life until He has first showed you His plan. God simply cannot take you to a place that you cannot see!

Now we know that as far as his natural vision was concerned, Abraham could not see beyond a couple of yards. So it is obvious that when God said, "the land which you see I give…" He was not referring to what Abraham could see with his physical eye. Rather, He was referring to what Abraham could perceive with his spiritual sight. Before Abraham could receive God's promise, he had to first see it through the eyes of his spirit.

Beloved, I am glad to announce to you that God has a great plan for your life. In Jeremiah 29:11, He says, *"I alone know the plans I have for you, plans to bring you prosperity and not disaster, plans to bring about the future you hope for"* (GNT). Yet, like Abraham, to receive God's plan, you must first see it. When you *see*, God will *do*. He will perform all His good promises and plans for you.

> Then the LORD said to me, "You have seen well, for I am ready to perform My word."
>
> JEREMIAH 1:12

The best time to dream is when you are in desperate need of a solution. You have heard it said many times: *"Necessity is the mother of invention."* Creativity functions best in the face of a need. Remember, Edison first saw the need for a safer more functional form of lighting. This inspired him to invent the incandescent electric light and an electric lighting system that contained all the elements necessary to make it practical, safe, and economical.

> When you "see," God will "do."

Are you facing a pressing need in your life? Please do not be *intimidated* by your need. Instead, be *inspired* by it. The time of need is not the time to *despair*. It is the time to *dream*. It is the time to see beyond the realm of the ordinary. It is the time to engage your spiritual vision and see into the realm of God's divine supply.

I encourage you, whatever need you may be facing at this time, see beyond the present difficulty and have a vision of the promise of God. God's Word contains the solution to every human problem. His Word has promises for any need, name it…health needs, financial needs, relationship needs…and so forth.

> Do not be **intimidated** by your need. Instead, be **inspired** by it!

Locate the portion of the Word of God that addresses your need. Begin to see your situation in the light of God's Word. If you have a health need, God says that by the stripes of Jesus you have **already** been healed. So see yourself as healed. Envision yourself doing the things that you could not do. See yourself out of your hospital bed. As you visualize God's solution, God will make your dreams and visions a reality. When you *see,* God will *do.*

Like the eagle, take full advantage of your area of acute vision. Maximize your spiritual eyes to see everything that God has destined for you. Look beyond your present circumstances and have a vision of a brighter future. Through supernatural sight, take steps of faith even when things look contrary in the natural.

And as you see, you will receive. You will overcome every earthly limitation. You will gain speed and acceleration in all that you do. You will no longer be grounded in the race of life. God will most definitely perform His good word concerning you.

THE EAGLE IS EXTREMELY PATIENT.

Eagles are remarkably patient birds. This truth is seen in the painstaking way in which an eagle hunts its prey. An eagle is known to roost for hours on end above a place where its prey has been spotted. It knows that if it makes any premature move, it may miss its target and lose its game.

So the eagle, defying its hunger, willingly waits for the right moment to strike. Its patience is often rewarded when its prey, unaware that the eagle is still present, comes out from its hiding place. The eagle then makes a swift descent upon its prey in one powerful one hundred mile-per-hour swoop.

Just as an eagle's hunting success largely depends on his ability to be patient, so also our success as believers is greatly determined by patience. You cannot be a person of great power and faith without being a person of equally great patience. The combination of faith and patience is vital in receiving anything from God. Hebrews 6:12 says, *"through faith and patience inherit the promises."*

> The combination of faith and patience is vital in receiving anything from God.

Without patience, the power of faith would be in vain. Many believers have missed out on God's blessings because they have not embraced the virtue of patience. They want *microwave miracles* and easily get discouraged when they feel that God has not acted as fast as they would have wanted. Hence they give up just mere seconds before their miracle arrives.

If you want God's best, you must be willing to pay the price of patience. Just as the eagle would lose its prey if he failed to be patient, without patience, you simply cannot gain the promises of God.

In the early 1990s, I knew a precious sister who through faith and patience *inherited* a wonderful husband from the Lord. At the time, she was in her 40s and had trusted the Lord for a spouse for a long time. Year after year, she watched ladies who were much younger than her get married. She witnessed her single girlfriends happily file down the marriage altar one after the other. Yet, she never felt bitter, disappointed, or frustrated. She maintained a cheerful disposition. She rejoiced and celebrated with others. She was one of the most diligent workers in church. Her lips were always full of praise and adoration to God.

Many in her situation would have given up on God. They would have turned their backs on Him and taken matters into their own hand. Many would have compromised their faith and backslidden because they felt betrayed by God. As a matter of fact, I personally knew a lady in a similar situation that was so desperate to get married and disappointed that God was *too slow* that she almost married a non-Christian.

But this was not the case with this dear patient sister. As the years continued to roll by, and it seemed as if she would remain an "old maid" for life, she refused to be bothered or consumed by her need for a husband. Instead, she chose to stay focused on God. She kept loving and serving God, remaining firm and strong in her faith. She held on to her dream for Mr. Right because she knew Whom she had believed. She was confident of God's faithfulness. She understood that times and seasons belonged to God alone. In His own appointed time He would surely bring to her the man of her dreams. God would never let her down.

Her faith and patience were rewarded when in her mid-40s she got an overseas job offer. To cut a long story short, it was during this year that she met her long-awaited husband. And he was certainly worth the wait. He was all that she had desired in a man and more. What's more, contrary to medical conventional wisdom that says that older women have a lesser chance to conceive, she got pregnant shortly after her marriage. Today, both she and her husband have a beautiful baby girl. They are still deeply in love and serve the Lord. Surely, good things come to those who wait…to those who wait patiently upon the Lord.

Beloved, are you trusting God for one miracle or the other? Are you tired of waiting and on the verge of giving up? If so, I plead with you, please do not throw in the towel. Like the eagle, you need to be patient.

> For ye have need of patience, that, after ye have done the will of God, ye might receive the promise.
>
> HEBREWS 10:36 (KJV)

Perhaps one of the greatest testimonies to an eagle's patience and determination is the meticulous way in which it builds its nest. Building a nest on a high mountain is undoubtedly more challenging than building one on a lower plane. Yet, the eagle goes about this tough job with amazing endurance.

The eagle patiently builds in the face of unbelievable hazards. Even in the event that the nest becomes destroyed, the eagle would determinedly start rebuilding. Col Stringer in his amazing book, *On Eagle's Wings*, writes:

An eagle's nest is a sight to behold. Usually perched high in the mountains, on the face of some sheer cliff or rock wall or the highest tree about, the nest is located in the most remote unattainable spot that he can find. The nest can be so huge that it will support two grown men. In fact, the nest itself can weigh in excess of two tons. Now remembering that each and every solitary stick has to be carried to this remote building site by the eagle, one can get some idea of the monumental size of the task. The eagle remodels the nest each year until it may hold thousands of sticks as well as timber from construction sites and discarded clothing and paper. Should the nest become dirty, fresh sticks, grace and leaves are carried up and piled on top of the old floor.

> Good things always come to those who wait...on God!

When things get difficult, and you feel like giving up, remember that tough times never last, only tough people do. You are not weak. You are tough. You are an eagle of God. You are destined to outlast your troubling situation. It will pass away, but you will stay strong and victorious because you are an eagle of God.

When things get tough, the tough get going! Like the eagle, choose to patiently persevere against all odds. Do not give up, because your miracle is on the way. Delay does not mean denial. God's time is the best. And He is always on time. As you saw in the case of the eagle, patience is always rewarded. Good things always come to those who wait…on God!

THE EAGLE IS SINGLE-MINDED.

Closely related to the eagle's virtue of patience is its single-mindedness. The eagle is a patient bird because it is an extremely focused bird. Once an eagle has a set goal, he sticks with his purpose until it is accomplished. For instance, nothing can distract an eagle when he is diving in for prey. When the eagle makes his catch, he firmly locks his prey in his talons holding on tightly and not letting it go.

As a matter of fact, an eagle would rather die than to release his hold on its prey. It has been reported that eagles, which drowned while trying

> Do not **under any circumstance** let go of God's promise!

to catch large fish, have been known to wash on the shore with their prey still firmly locked in their talons. Not even the threat of death could make the eagle release its hold.

In like manner, as an eagle Christian, you must have a firm grip on the Word of God. Nothing should ever make you let go of your faith in the Lord. Do not let anything make you stop believing God. In the face of contrary winds, hold on firmly to the confidence that you have placed in God's Word.

> Therefore do not cast away your confidence, which has great reward.
>
> HEBREWS 10:35

Do not **under any circumstance** let go of God's promise. Get to the point where you say, *"I burn all my bridges. I put aside all my options. I refuse to have any alternatives. If God does not do it, let it not be done."*

Years ago, my wife was at this point. For years she had battled a very stubborn case of malaria fever that would come at a particular time of the year. About the same time, every single year, she would come down with a tough bout of the disease. Even worse was the fact that she had a very bad allergic reaction to its medicine. According to her, the reaction to the cure for malaria was worse than the disease itself.

Then one day she got a hold of God's Word that said, "By His stripes you were healed." She figured that if God said she was healed, malaria had no right to invade her body year in, year out. She chose to hold on tenaciously to God's Word and braced herself to resist any future malaria attack.

Well, sure enough, at the set time of the year, she came down with the disease. But this time, instead of staying down, she chose to rise up strong in faith, persistently holding on to God's promise for her healing. For days, the symptoms continued, yet she held on to God's promise. Though she ran over 100-degree body temperature, and had aches and pains all over, she refused to stay in bed. Instead, she rose up and went about her usual duties.

She *behaved* as if she were healed because she *believed* that she was already healed. At one point she said, "Lord, I will not let go of Your Word even if it means I must die." Talk about being single-minded!

Eventually after about a week, all the symptoms disappeared. She was miraculously and totally delivered from the recurring fever by the healing power of God.

Many people do not succeed in life because they get impatient and double-minded. If you break your focus, and start considering "alternatives" to God's Word, you cannot receive anything from Him (*James 1:6-8*).

Like the eagle, God wants you to be single-minded toward Him and your assignments. Stay focused on whatever it is God has commanded you to do. Stay focused on the Word of God. Every challenge of life will pass away. It is only the Word of God that will remain (*Matthew 5:18*). So stand firm upon His Word and you will never be ashamed.

> For the LORD God will help Me; Therefore I will not be disgraced; Therefore I have set My face like a flint, and I know that I will not be ashamed.
>
> ISAIAH 50:7

Remember, a broken focus is often the reason why people fail in the pursuit of their life's assignment. It is the reason why God's promises are not finding expression in the life of many Christians today. Please do not become its victim. Be single-minded toward God. When things get tough and complicated, do not shift your focus away from His Word and try to do something easier. No! You are an eagle. You are seated in heavenly places. You can handle any situation. You have dominion!

CHAPTER SEVENTEEN

ASCEND YOUR THRONE!

Each covenant placement that we have studied—the sheep, lion, son, and eagle positions—can be compared to the four legs of a throne. Just as the legs of a physical chair help keep its seat sturdy and secure, so also each *leg* of your heavenly throne is extremely important.

Consider this: If just one leg of a chair is broken or removed, regardless of the fact that the other three are still intact, it would not stand upright. The stability of the chair would immediately be threatened.

Similarly, if you want to position yourself for dominion and take your seat in the heavenly places, you must give top consideration and attention to these four facets of your covenant position in Christ. Do not focus on one or two positions and then disregard the others. You must fully understand and embrace all four aspects of your covenant position. Only then will you be able to walk in dominion and reign as the king that God made you to be.

As I mentioned earlier, the first and foremost thing that you must understand is that you are a sheep of God. If you want to reign, you must first be redeemed. However, while it is fundamental for you to take your position as a sheep of God, you need to understand that the other positions are very important as well. You need to have a complete and working understanding of all four covenant positions if you would walk in absolute (not partial) dominion. Remember: **Dominion is your crown of glory, Dominion is your conquering power, and Dominion is your divine capability.**

For instance, God wants you to mature in your sonship authority so that you can reign supreme as a king in the earth. Remember, *only mature sons ascend thrones.* Only as a grown son of God can you exert authority and receive the fullness of your inheritance in Christ. Simply put, **it is only as a son that you can experience dominion as your crown of glory.**

Again, it is not God's will for you to fall prey to satan's attacks. He has ordained you as a lion of God that puts the enemy to flight. You are the devil's super-predator; he is your prey. Simply put, **Dominion is the conquering power that God has given you to subdue the enemy under your feet.**

Last but definitely not the least, God has ordained you to be an eagle so that you can always soar high in the race of life. He does not want you to struggle. He wants you to excel in life and make an indelible mark for Christ for many generations. He says, *"I will make you an eternal excellence, a joy of many generations" (Isaiah 60:15b). So,* **Dominion is your divine capability to succeed and be a flyer in the race of life.**

Do you get it? Do you now see how the various aspects of your covenant position connect with the three basic elements of Dominion? Today, many of God's own righteous people are suffering because they lack a complete understanding of who they are in Christ. They only have a partial knowledge of who they are in Christ. Please understand that partial understanding brings partial dominion. If you want to experience absolute dominion in every aspect of life, you must have a complete understanding of your covenant position in Christ.

For instance, you may understand that you are a sheep Christian. You may be sensitive and obedient to the voice of God. Yet

> Partial understanding brings partial dominion!

without the boldness, courage and strength of a lion, you will not be in a position to carry out God's commands in the face of a tough situation. You will not be able to do exploits for Him.

Moreover, without courage, you cannot confront and overcome the enemy in battle. This explains why so many precious saints seem to be harassed and troubled by the devil today. They suffer at the hands of the evil one, not because they have committed any sin, not because they have disobeyed God, but rather because they have not learned how to operate as a lion of God. They watch passively as the devil harasses them on every side.

> Many of God's own righteous people are suffering because they lack a complete understanding of who they are in Christ.

There are yet others who have understood what it means to be a sheep Christian, yet they have not yet discovered how to function in their sonship and eagle authority. Such Christians are likely to live mediocre or average lives. They live far below the potential that God has placed in them. Typically, such believers are content just to be God's sheep, and go to heaven when they die.

In my case, in the early days of my walk with God, I largely focused on my position as a sheep of God. I did not understand that I was also a lion, son, and eagle of God. Due to my ignorance, I suffered miserably at the hands of the devil. Hosea 4:6 says, "My people are destroyed for lack of knowledge." It was not until I began to understand and operate in all aspects of my covenant position—as a sheep, lion, son and eagle— that I experienced true power and victory in life.

Beloved, you are a highly placed individual. In Christ, God has made you a sheep, lion, son, and an eagle. You are seated together in heavenly places in Christ far above every force of darkness.

Seated together in Jesus, you possess the exact same power by which He healed the sick, raised the dead, and cast out devils. He has given you that power, which He used so mightily while He walked the earth. By His authority, you, too, can reign in life and overcome all the evil schemes of the devil just as He did:

Behold, I give you the authority to trample on serpents and scorpions, and over all the power of the enemy, and nothing shall by any means hurt you.

LUKE 10:19

Today many believers are not *ascending* their thrones. Instead, they are *abdicating* their heavenly seats! They are not enforcing their dominion authority. They are not ruling and reigning. They are not excelling.

> Many believers are not ascending their thrones. Instead, they are abdicating their heavenly seats!

But this does not have to be the case with you. Now you know who you are. You understand the power and privileges that you possess as a sheep, lion, son, and eagle of God. So put your knowledge to work.

Refuse to be a "punching bag" in the hand of the devil. You do not have to be bombarded and barraged by one calamity after the other. You do not have to suffer setback upon setback. Take your place in the heavenlies. Give full attention to all four facets of your covenant position. Live like the sheep, son, lion, and eagle that God has made you to be. Walk in dominion every single day of your life!

PART THREE

HINDRANCES TO DOMINION

For you did not receive **the spirit of bondage again to fear**, but you received the Spirit of adoption by whom we cry out, "Abba, Father."

ROMANS 8:15

Chapter Eighteen

Fear—The Archenemy of Dominion

For you did not receive **the spirit of bondage again to fear**, but you received the Spirit of adoption by whom we cry out, "Abba, Father."

ROMANS 8:15

For God has not given us a spirit of fear, but of power and of love and of a sound mind.

2 TIMOTHY 1:7

One of the things that will cause a believer to abdicate his God-given heavenly seat is fear. Fear will hinder a Christian from ascending his throne and reigning in life. A fearful believer cannot walk in dominion. This is because fear is a spirit of bondage, which enslaves and subdues its victim.

The words *fear* and *bondage* go together. Where there is fear, there will be bondage. And it is impossible for a person who is in bondage to walk in dominion. Many in Christ Jesus desire to walk in dominion but are crippled and bound by the debilitating spirit of fear.

Fear is a destiny destroyer. It humiliates and intimidates. As long as a person is ruled by fear, he will not reach his full potential in God. Fear makes a believer a victim of life while faith makes him a victor in life. In short, fear is the archenemy of dominion.

As a matter of fact, every single gift that God has in store for you is received by faith, but rejected by fear. Yes, it is true! Anytime you give in to fear, you shut the door against the power and promise of God for your life. No one has ever gained anything by fear. Fear only comes to take from you. *With faith all things are possible, but with fear nothing is possible.*

THE ORIGIN OF FEAR

The best way to solve a problem is to deal with it directly from its root. When you understand fear's origin, you will be in a better position to overcome it. Many have tried to win their battle with fear, but have been unsuccessful because they had merely attacked it from the surface.

> Fear makes a believer a victim of life. But faith will make him a victor in life.

For instance, there are some who erroneously think that fear is only an emotion or feeling. As a result, they try to tackle it with human psychology. This will do no good because fear is not a psychological state of mind. It is a tormenting spirit.

> There is no fear in love; but perfect love casts out fear, because fear involves torment. But he who fears has not been made perfect in love.

1 JOHN 4:8

Fear is a spirit that originated from the pit of hell. The devil is the number-one producer and instiller of fear. And to understand how fear came into our earthly realm, we must go back to the dawn of human history—to the Garden of Eden. The first time the word *fear* is mentioned in Scripture it is in association with Adam, shortly after his fall.

> Then the LORD God called to Adam and said to him, "Where are you?" So he said, "I heard Your voice in the garden, and I was afraid because I was naked; and I hid myself."

GENESIS 3:9-10

Before the fall of man, fear was absent from Eden. But as soon as man sinned, fear came in. Sin opened the door to the evil spirit of fear. So satan is the originator of fear, and sin is its access gate.

The devil is always out to sabotage God's plan for your life. He will try to undermine your dominion by instilling fear in you. He instills fear through various forms:

- **Through evil spirits** that greatly torment an individual with diverse kinds of phobias. This is an extreme and strange level of fear that literally controls and grips its victim ceaselessly.

- **Through dangerous environments** created by the havoc that satan wreaks in society, such as terrorist attacks or threats, crime, hazards, etc.

- **Through negative cultural influences** such as bad entertainment (horror movies, thrillers, etc), which has helped to produce in our society a culture of fear.

- **Through human agents.** These are wicked, sadistic people who take delight in making others feel afraid. They frighten the weak and helpless with proud, intimidating, and boastful words. Some of these people may be directly or indirectly involved with the enemy through satanic cults and associations.

However, you do not have to be intimidated by the devil in any shape or form by which he brings fear. You do not have to give in to fear because God did not give you the spirit of fear.

> For you did not receive **the spirit of bondage again to fear**, but you received the Spirit of adoption by whom we cry out, "Abba, Father."
>
> ROMANS 8:15

God has not given you any form of fear. So do not embrace it. On the contrary, He has given you the Spirit of adoption—His Holy Spirit. Through His Spirit, He made you a part of His family. And because you are born of God, you can overcome fear.

> For whatever is born of God overcomes the world. And this is the victory that has overcome the world—our faith.
>
> 1 JOHN 5:4

Every battle of life is won by faith, but lost by fear. Fear has absolutely nothing to offer you. It is one of the enemy's strongest weapons by which he seeks to steal, kill, and destroy the saints of God. This is how devastating fear is.

Beloved, you dare not give it any chance in your life. This is because it is impossible for a person to be full of faith when he is full of fear. Remember God has not given you a spirit of fear. You have the Spirit of God. You have His authority and dominion.

FEAR REPRODUCES ITSELF.

Just as faith produces God's good plans, fear produces the devil's evil purposes. In this sense, fear actually reproduces after the likeness or nature of satan, its originator. The devil is wicked and full of hatred for mankind. Through fear he carries out his evil plans in a person's life. While faith delivers the promises of God, fear delivers the perils of the devil.

Just as you can **have what you believe** God for, quite often **people have what they are afraid of**. Yes, it is true! A person may ultimately experience the very calamity or trouble that he had feared. This is why you should steer clear of fear. If left unconquered, today's fears may become tomorrow's realities. This is because fear actually reproduces itself.

> Just as you can have what you believe God for, quite often people have what they are afraid of. **This is why you** should steer clear of **fear!**

My wife experienced this shocking fact in 1980 while traveling with her entire family. They were returning back home after her grandfather's memorial service. They were all tired, and everyone except her and her father (who was driving) was sleeping through the journey.

Suddenly, for no apparent reason she was overcome by an enormous feeling of fear. Her fears were heightened by an equally terrifying thought that constantly barraged her mind. This was the thought: *"Fall asleep and your father will fall asleep and then you will all have an accident."*

Now, my wife was not yet born again at the time. Apparently, she did not know how to deal with the deadly spirit that had now enveloped her. As best as she could, she tried to fight off the thoughts while trying to stay awake at the same time. Then suddenly, without warning, she heard a loud bang, and was simultaneously jolted out of her seat. They had been hit by an eighteen-wheeler and their car was suddenly spinning out of control.

On both sides of the narrow road lay deep ravines covered with sharp, jagged rocks. Should their car fall into the depths that would mean certain death for them all. Her father struggled to gain control of the car, which kept swerving because of the tremendous impact.

After a few moments, and by God's special grace, the car came to a screeching halt. When they got out of the car, they discovered that its right side was completely totaled. However, miraculously, no one was hurt.

For a long time the whole ordeal remain etched in my wife's memory. She shuddered as she pondered on how her fears actually became reality. How terrible is the destructive reproductive ability of fear! Job admitted that it was the very thing that he feared which came upon him. He said, "…the thing I was afraid of has come upon me…"

> For the thing I greatly feared has come upon me, and what I dreaded has happened to me. I am not at ease, nor am I quiet; I have no rest, for trouble comes.
>
> JOB 3:25-26

The fear of failure brings failure. Many people are sick today because they were afraid of sickness. Many are poor because they were afraid of poverty. It is strange but it is true. You may end up experiencing everything that you fear. Moreover, if you live in constant fear of tomorrow, you will not enjoy today. So steer clear of fear!

Have you faced, or are you currently facing strong and fearful opposition from the enemy? Well, I am glad to announce to you that you are much stronger than he.

> When a strong man, fully armed, guards his own palace, his goods are in peace. But when a stronger than he comes upon him and overcomes him, he takes from him all his armor in which he trusted, and divides his spoils.
>
> *LUKE 11:21-22*

Change your mentality about the devil. In Christ, you have the power to overcome fear and overthrow all the works of the devil. Though the storms seem to rage all around you…. FEAR NOT! You are the stronger one.

FEAR THRIVES ON DECEPTION.

Someone once defined fear as—False Evidence Appearing Real. This is so true.

> Every battle of life is won by faith, but lost by fear.

In Florida, on November 2, 1995, a man who was angry about some immigration problems that he was having, forced a woman and child onto a school bus that was carrying a group of children and teachers and then hijacked it. He had a bag, which he claimed contained a bomb. For hours he terrorized his hostages who truly believed that he had a bomb and would blow up the bus should they make any attempt to resist him. Eventually after a long police chase, the hijacker was killed and the frightened hostages rescued.

However when the police opened the bag, presumably to diffuse the deadly weapon, they discovered that the bag did not contain a bomb as he had alleged. The entire hijack had been based on a lie. He had deceived his hostages into believing that he had a bomb so that they would not try to resist or subdue him.

Now, what if the bus driver or any of the teachers knew the truth? What if they knew, right from the beginning, that the hijacker was lying? I truly believe that if they knew that he did not have a bomb, and he was not as powerful as he made himself out to be, their reaction would have been very different. They would not have allowed him to hold them hostage. The man was clearly outnumbered. They would have brought him down in a heartbeat!

What happened that fateful day in Florida gives us a clear picture of how the devil operates in the lives of fearful believers today. Like the phony hijacker, the devil does not have the capacity to destroy you or blow up your destiny.

Though he goes about fuming and threatening you; though he fills your mind with fearful thoughts and nightmares; you need to know that he is not as powerful as he makes himself out to be. He is all bark and no bite. Jesus has completely stripped him of the power to harm or hurt you.

> Having wiped out the handwriting of requirements that was against us, which was contrary to us. And He has taken it out of the way, hav-

ing nailed it to the cross. Having disarmed principalities and powers, He made a public spectacle
of them, triumphing over them in it.

COLOSSIANS 2:14-15

One of the first things that a conquering army does to its
prisoners of war is to seize their weapons. After they have
disarmed their prisoners, they then put them in confine-
ment. That way, the conquerors are sure that their POWs
will not pose any threat to them.

The devil is our Lord's prisoner of war! Yes, that is all
that satan is. he is not a conqueror. he is a **conquered foe**.
Don't you ever forget it! Jesus defeated the devil hands
down. satan has ZERO power over you. Jesus has completely disarmed him. he cannot harm you. he cannot pose
a threat to you or stop you from prospering. he simply cannot hinder you from excelling and reigning in life.

You, on the other hand, have DOMINION. You have
been greatly empowered by Jesus to Whom belongs
ALL power.

And Jesus came and spake unto them, saying, All power is given unto me in heaven
and in earth.

MATTHEW 28:18 (KJV)

Can you now see that you have no reason whatsoever
to be afraid of the devil? Though you should be vigilant
and on the alert for his evil activities (*1 Peter 5:8*) ...

though you should be aware of his pranks and schemes (*2 Corinthians 2:11*), you should never, ever be afraid of him. Never!

There is no device or plan of satan that you cannot undo. No weapon that he forms against you shall prosper. No purpose of his can stand. God's Word is clear—you have power over all his power. You have dominion.

When a person embraces fear, he or she is indirectly saying, "I believe in the ability of the devil to hurt, more than I believe in the power of God's hand to save." Please, do not fall into this error. Understand that the Bible never calls satan a mighty devil or a powerful devil. On the contrary, the Bible says—All power belongs to God. Now, if all power belongs to God, what then is left for the devil? Nothing!

> God has spoken once, twice I have heard this:
> That power belongs to God.
>
> *PSALM 62:11*

So you need to understand that the devil is not as powerful as he makes himself out to be. Did you notice what 1 Peter 5:8 says? It says that the devil goes about "like a roaring lion." This means that the devil pretends to be a roaring lion, but in reality he is not. But you have the real Lion living on the inside of you. Jesus, the Lion of the tribe of Judah, in you is greater than all the forces of hell combined.

SATAN IS THE SLYEST CON MAN EVER!

While the Bible does not refer to the devil as powerful, it does call him a man of devices or tricks. In his first appearance in the Scriptures (Genesis 3:1,4), he is portrayed as a cunning man, a man of tricks, a deceiver. **Not** as a man of power.

As a matter of fact, by virtue of their dominion authority, Adam and Eve were more powerful than the devil. The devil knew he stood no chance against them. So instead of coming against them with strength, he confronted man with subtlety.

Trickery and deceit is the devil's mindset. He is a deceiver who goes about deceiving people even up till today. And he will continue to use deceit till his time is up.

> He performs great signs, so that he even makes fire come down from heaven on the earth in the sight of men. And he deceives those who dwell on the earth by those signs which he was granted to do in the sight of the beast, telling those who dwell on the earth to make an image to the beast who was wounded by the sword and lived.
>
> REVELATION 13:13-14

> Then I saw an angel coming down from heaven, having the key to the bottomless pit and a great chain in his hand. He laid hold of the dragon, that serpent of old, who is the

Devil and Satan, and bound him for a thousand years; and he cast him into the bottomless pit, and shut him up, and set a seal on him, so that he should deceive the nations no more till the thousand years were finished. But after these things he must be released for a little while.

REVELATION 20:1-3

Through his lies, he blindfolds the mind of the unsaved from the truth of the gospel. Many times he uses the blindfold of logic, intellectualism, false religion, and so forth to keep men from seeing and believing the truth of God's Word.

But even if our gospel is veiled, it is veiled to those who are perishing, whose minds the god of this age has blinded, who do not believe, lest the light of the gospel of the glory of Christ, who is the image of God, should shine on them.

2 CORINTHIANS 4:3-4

Through his evil devices, the devil also deceives and takes advantage of ignorant believers. For instance he uses the tool of "religion" to prevent believers from enjoying everything that God has for them. By his lies he has succeeded in keeping countless number of Christians in the bondage of the fear of poverty, pain, and all manner of peril. Believe it or not, some believers are actually afraid that their God-given prosperity would make them backslide.

he has lied to others, telling them that the days of healing are long gone and that it is not God's will for them to be healed. So they choose not to believe God for their healing because they are afraid that if they do they would be disappointed. They choose instead to remain as they are—sick, dejected, and discouraged. But these are all lies of the devil. Poverty, sickness, and struggling are not synonymous with righteousness. God *does* want you to prosper in all things (2 Corinthians 8:9; 3 John 2).

> The most vulnerable Christian is an ignorant one.
> If the devil cannot trick you, he cannot triumph over you through fear.

If you want to walk in dominion, you must not be ignorant of satan's mindset of deceit. When you know how the enemy thinks and operates, he will never be able to take advantage of you. he will not have the upper hand in your life.

Lest satan take advantage of us; for we are not ignorant of his devices.

2 CORINTHIANS 2:11

Ignorant believers, because they lack the knowledge of the power of God that they possess, have often time given the devil undue credit. Sadly, some believers live in fear of his activities. They believe in what the devil can do against them more than what God can do for them. How sad! Through fear, they *blow the devil's trumpet* when they really should be *boasting* about God's power.

Beloved, do not be deceived. Do not be ignorant of the evil scheming of the devil or else he will take advantage of you. The most vulnerable Christian is an ignorant one. Remember, if you know your enemy and you know yourself, you are guaranteed of 100-percent victory over the enemy all the time. But if you know your enemy, yet do not know yourself; or you know yourself but do not know your enemy, you only have a 50/50 chance of winning. And if you neither know yourself nor your enemy you have absolutely no chance of victory in battle.

When you know your enemy and his ways, you will not fall for his lies. Take note of this fact: If the devil cannot trick you, he cannot triumph over you through fear. For instance, God's Word tells us that the fear of death brings bondage.

> Inasmuch then as the children have partaken of flesh and blood, He Himself likewise shared in the same, that through death He might destroy him who had the power of death, that is, the devil, and release those who through fear of death were all their lifetime subject to bondage.
>
> HEBREWS 2:14-15

But when you know the truth about death, that it has lost its sting, you will no longer live in fear of death. You will be full of faith in the power of God's Word. You will not live in fear of the future. You will not be troubled about whether evil will come to you or your loved ones. Rather, your heart will be steadfast, trusting in the Lord (Psalm 112:7).

Friend, in life's battles, remember that satan, your enemy, is not omnipresent, omniscient, or omnipotent. But God is! The devil is limited, but your God in you is not! God is everywhere, He knows everything, and He can do all things. He is with you as a Mighty Terrible One. And because the Omnipresent, Omniscient, Omnipotent God is for you, no devil in the pit of hell can be against you.

God knows the fears that confront you in the world, He knows what you should do to combat them, and He has given you dominion authority to conquer the enemy. So shake yourself free from the deadly shackles of fear. Make up your mind to live a fear-free life. Walk in dominion over every fear of the enemy.

CHAPTER NINETEEN
WHAT YOU MUST DO TO
CONQUER FEAR

In the epic film, *The King and I*, when asked by her son Louis about how to handle fear, Anna Leonowns responded with a song: *"Whenever I feel afraid I hold my head erect and whistle a happy tune so no one will suspect I am afraid."*

Well, that formula is only good for the movies. In the real world, you know that you cannot defeat fear by whistling or merely singing a song. Like I said earlier on, fear is more than a disturbing emotion. It is a tormenting sprit. As a result, it cannot be overcome by natural means. You cannot conquer fear through sheer human will power. Neither can you overcome fear by putting up a show of confidence.

In contrast to Anna's theory, in Psalm 56:3-4, the Bible shows you **what you should really do whenever you are afraid.**

Whenever I am afraid, **I will trust in You**. In God (**I will praise His Word**), In God I have put my trust; I will not fear. What can flesh do to me?

PSALM 56:3-4

God's answer is clear. Whenever you are tempted to be afraid, choose to trust in God. Have faith in Him— fear not! *Praise* His Word. Only believe God's report. *Overcome fear by your faith.* Faith gives you access to the realm of divine security.

What is faith? Faith is having absolute confidence in God's Word. **Faith is having confidence in the greatness of God that good things will always happen to you.** *Faith is the expectation of good not of evil.* When you have faith in God, you will not expect bad things to happen to you.

You see, anytime you are faced with a troubling situation, you will always have two options. You can either choose to be afraid of the circumstance or you can choose to reverence God by having faith in Him. You must choose one or the other. You cannot have it both ways. It is either you choose to be afraid of the terror around you, or you choose to fear the Lord. There are no in-betweens.

> **Faith is having confidence in the greatness of God that good things will always happen to you.** Faith is the expectation of good not of evil!

If you choose to be afraid of the circumstance, then you will end up becoming its victim. Remember fear reproduces itself. On the other hand, if you choose to fear the Lord and place your trust in Him, you will be victorious over your trial. Make God your confidence, and you will enjoy His security, rest, joy, and peace.

> Do not be afraid of sudden terror, Nor of trouble from the wicked when it comes; For the LORD will be your confidence, and will keep your foot from being caught.
>
> PROVERBS 3:25-26

Your faith in the Lord is a reflection of your love for Him. When you love Him, you will be devoted to Him. You will seek to please Him in all things; you will walk uprightly and righteously before Him. And the easiest way to command divine security and enviable prosperity is to love Him with all your heart.

> Because you have made the LORD, who is my refuge, even the Most High, your dwelling place, no evil shall befall you, nor shall any plague come near your dwelling; For He shall give His angels charge over you, to keep you in all your ways. In their hands they shall bear you up, lest you dash your foot against a stone. You shall tread upon the lion and the cobra, the young lion and the serpent you shall trample underfoot. **"Because he has set his love upon Me, therefore I will deliver him; I will set him on high, because he has known My name. He shall call upon Me, and I will answer him; I**

will be with him in trouble; I will deliver him and honor him. With long life I will satisfy him, and show him My salvation."

PSALM 91:9-16

God's joy and pleasure is to be believed. Your faith and confidence in God is proof that you really love Him. It is only faith in Him that will produce the miracles and breakthroughs you desire. Faith is the only voice that God respects and responds to. God literally scans the whole earth, looking for those who have loyal and trusting hearts toward Him. To such people, God will show Himself strong. He will move mightily on the behalf of those who have faith in Him (*2 Chronicles 16:9; James 1: 6-8*).

PRAISE HIS WORD

Anytime you are in a tough situation, do not panic. Instead, *praise God's Word*. Everything on earth must bow to the supremacy of God's Word. Heaven and earth will pass away but not one jot or title in God's Word will go without being fulfilled. If you choose to praise His Word—if you choose to place your faith in the supremacy of God's Word—whatever it is you are facing will pass. Only God's good Word for you will remain.

> Anytime you are in a tough situation, do not panic. Instead, praise God's Word.

God is happy when you trust Him. What pleases Him most is when you place your absolute faith in His Word (*Hebrews 11: 6*).

Beloved, it pays to believe God. You have nothing to lose when you place your faith in Him. There is no situation too hopeless for God to fix. There is nothing too hard or impossible for Him to do. And if you believe Him, if you reverence Him with your faith, nothing shall be impossible for you, too *(Matthew 17:20)*.

FEAR NOT, ONLY BELIEVE

What can be more terrifying and hopeless than the loss of a child? In the eighth chapter of the gospel according to Luke, we read about the story of Jairus, a respected ruler in Israel. He faced the most fearsome experience of his life when his daughter who had been gravely ill, died.

While she was still alive, in his desperation he had sought the Master to come and heal his sick child. However, before Jesus arrived at his house, his daughter had died. At this point as far as Jairus was concerned, there was no hope. He thought he would never see his little girl again.

Jesus, seeing the despair and hopelessness in his eyes, said, *"Do not be afraid; only believe, and she will be made well."* He was quick to remind Jairus that in his troubling situation he had two options: He could both reverence God by his faith and believe Him for a miracle, or he could give in to the spirit of fear.

Jesus encouraged him to go with the first option. In essence Jesus was saying, *"Jairus, I know that what you are looking at is fearful, but do not react in fear. Reverence Me by your faith. Do not allow the frightful sight of your stone dead daughter to overcome you with despair. Replace your fears with faith. Praise My Word. And all will be well."*

Well, you know what happened next. Jesus laid His hands on the dead child and commanded life to return back to her. In an instant, a seemingly hopeless situation turned around for good all because fear was replaced by faith.

WALK BY FAITH AND YOU WILL WALK IN DOMINION.

Do you want to be immune to the fears that plague others? Do you want to experience victory and mastery over every storm of life? Then have faith in God. Do not magnify the problem. Instead *praise God's Word.*

Do what Jesus did in the face of a raging storm. By His bold declaration of God's Word, He took dominion authority over the raging winds, and the sea became calm. His disciples on the other hand had reacted in fear. They chose to be terrified instead of trusting the Lord. For this, Jesus rebuked them saying, "Why are you so fearful? How is it that you have no faith?" (Mark 4:35-41).

When you exalt God's Word in reverential fear, every storm of your life will be silenced. Then you will not be terrified of your enemies. There will be absolutely no room in your heart for the fear of the enemy or his evil plans.

And not in any way terrified by your adversaries, which is to them a proof of perdition, but to you of salvation, and that from God.

PHILIPPIANS 1: 28

When storms of life confront you, do not fear the storm. Fear the Savior! Recognize the saving power of your God and place your total faith in Him. When you choose to fear the Lord, all other fears will lose their power over you. Get rid of the fear and enchantment mentality. As a believer, no enchantment can work against you. You are not a prey for the devil's consumption. You are a conqueror!

Like David, look at the fears of the world and confidently say,

"The LORD is my light and my salvation; Whom shall I fear? The LORD is the strength of my life; Of whom shall I be afraid? When the wicked came against me to eat up my flesh, my enemies and foes, they stumbled and fell. Though an army may encamp against me, my heart shall not fear; Though war should rise against me, in this I will be confident."

PSALM 27:1-3

When you have faith in the Lord you will constantly love and worship Him with all your heart. You will trust His Word completely in all things. You will know that no matter how unsafe and troubled the world becomes, your God is a solid rock, and in Him you will never be shaken!

Surely he will never be shaken; The righteous will be in everlasting remembrance. He will not be afraid of evil tidings; His heart is steadfast, trusting in the LORD. His heart is established; He will not be afraid, until he sees his desire upon his enemies.

PSALM 112:6-8

Fear creates and produces tragedies. But your faith in God will always deliver good things to you. It will put you over in all life's difficulties. Do not let your feelings guide or influence your response in trying situations. Do not allow what you hear on your local news station overwhelm you. Let God's Word be your only source of influence.

As our Lord Jesus said to Jairus, so say I to you in the midst of every "dead" situation that confronts you— Fear not, only believe and you will see the salvation of the Lord. Walk by faith. Do not walk by sight! Walk by faith, and you will walk in dominion!

CHAPTER TWENTY

TAKE ACTION AGAINST YOUR FEARS

For the turning away of the simple will slay them, and the complacency of fools will destroy them; **But whoever listens to me will dwell safely, and will be secure, without fear of evil**."

PROVERBS 1:32-33

I stated earlier that fear is reproductive in nature. If today's fears are not dealt with, they may become tomorrow's realities. This is why it is very important that you attack your fears with a passion.

Fear is not something that you live with or tolerate. It is a robber of destiny. *It is the archenemy of dominion.* As long as you are fearful, you will not experience absolute dominion in life. You simply cannot afford to be indifferent or complacent to fear. To do so is to foolishly court disaster—the complacency of fools will destroy them!

Most of the time satan will announce his evil plans by planting a fearful thought in your mind. He will bring fear of impending evil, calamity, and disease. Do not tolerate such thoughts for one moment. Take action against them immediately. To allow fearful thoughts to have a hold on your mind is to give the enemy an open door for attack. Do not be complacent or passive. Crush every fearful thought with the Word of God. Then satan's evil plans will not see the light of day.

> For the weapons of our warfare are not carnal, but mighty through God to the pulling down of strong holds; **Casting down imaginations**, and every high thing that exalteth itself against the knowledge of God, and **bringing into captivity every thought to the obedience of Christ**.

> *2 CORINTHIANS 10:4-5*

We live in an extremely dangerous world. Face it. There are countless reasons why anyone would be afraid in today's society. But you are not just anyone. If you are born again, you are no longer in the realm of ordinary men. You are in the realm of the Most High God! Seated with Him, you are positioned far above the enemy. The evil darts of the wicked one cannot reach you.

> He who comes from above is above all; he who is of the earth is earthly and speaks of the earth. He who comes from heaven is above all.

> *JOHN 3:31*

You belong to God Almighty. Do not to be afraid of the things that make others shake in fright. Though you live in the same perilous environment as the people of the world, do not be afraid of the things that make others tremble. Instead, have faith in God. Do not fear the spirit of fear. Fear God alone!

> "Do not say, 'A conspiracy,' concerning all that this people call a conspiracy, nor be afraid of their threats, nor be troubled. The LORD of hosts, Him you shall hallow; Let Him be your fear, and let Him be your dread."
>
> ISAIAH 8:11-13 (KJV)

What are the "fears" of the people of the world? Well, many are afraid of all kinds of terrorist's threats. We hear of the terror of possible biological, chemical, nuclear strikes on our land. Others are afraid of the world's unstable economy, rising unemployment, increasing crime rates, strange incurable diseases that are ravaging mankind...and the list goes on and on. In our world today, men's hearts are literally failing them for fear. Heart attacks are rapidly becoming the leading cause of death.

According to Isaiah 8, you will always overcome fear when you choose to fear the Lord. But what does this mean in practical terms? What definite steps must you take anytime you are confronted with fear? Here are four real ways to approach and arrest fear in your life:

1. RECOGNIZE FEAR: WHAT ARE YOU AFRAID OF?

The first step to overcoming any problem is admittance. Many people who are confronted with the spirit of fear do not want to own up to the fact that they are fearful. They are like the proverbial ostrich that buries his head in the ground whenever he is afraid. Instead of facing up to its fear, it hides from it.

But saying that something does not exist will not make it disappear. Unless you identify your fears, you will not be able to confront or conquer them.

Another reason why many deny that they have a problem with fear is that they feel that fear is normal. They feel it is natural to be worried or fretful, especially in today's society. They have accepted fear as a way of life and see no need to eliminate it. Many feel fear is a normal human emotion and so it should be tolerated.

This is not true! Fear is your worst enemy—it is the archenemy of your dominion. You must not give it a moment's place in your life. Fear enslaves, and slavery is not a normal state of being.

Over and over again in Scripture, we are commanded not to fear. If it were okay to be afraid, God would not command against it. So your first action against fear is to identify what exactly it is you are afraid of. Go to a quiet place and make a list of all the things that torment you with worry day after day. What are the things that make you jittery and fretful? What causes peace of mind to leave you?

It may be fear of failure, fear of sickness or disease, fear of some great danger like a natural disaster or terrorist attack. Some people, believe it or not, are afraid of success! As a result, they would rather remain mediocre than strive for greatness. The good news is, whatever it is you are afraid of, according to God's Word, you have the power to live above it!

2. Analyze Fear: Why Are You Afraid?

The next question you need to ask yourself is—why am I afraid? Nothing ever happens without a cause. This is called the law of cause and effect. Just as mosquito bites cause malaria, more often than not, real incidents, experiences, or influences are responsible for our fears.

Some people are afraid of dogs because, earlier in life, they had been bitten by a dog. Some are afraid of success because they know someone who was once successful but has now been brought low. Others are afraid because they have exposed their minds to the negativity that pervades today's entertainment world.

Think back and try to identify what triggered your fear. After you have identified the cause, then proceed to "cut" the supply line. By cutting the "supply line," I mean that you should sever yourself from what you have identified to be the source of your fear. Starve your fears, but feed your faith!

This may mean you may have to censor certain TV programs or movies. You may have to stop going to certain places. You may even have to cut yourself off from certain people. There are some people who are so pessimistic that if you continue to hang around them, you will have a gloomy and negative outlook to life.

Moreover, do not let what happened in someone else's life instill fear in you. Do not live your life in fear of someone else's bad experience. Remember the Bible says, "The just shall live by his own faith." Do not let the negative experience of another shake your faith. Just because something bad happened to somebody else does not mean that the same thing will happen to you.

3. TAKE ACTION: HOW WILL YOU CONFRONT YOUR FEARS?

It has been said, "Attack is the best form of defense." The next thing to do after you have identified the cause of your fears is to strike it first before it strikes you.

Fear is fierce in its onslaught. It is not passive. So you must make the first move and attack it ferociously. Look your fears squarely in the eye. Face up to them. Do not run away.

As you confront your fear, you will eventually control it. You will become its master. Fight fear with all your physical, moral, and spiritual strength. Never give in to fear.

Take a stand against fear by doing the exact things that you fear. **Do the things you fear, and the death of fear is certain!** If you do not do the things you fear, fear will continue to control your life. But if you confront fear by the power of God's Word, you will ultimately conquer it. Master your fear. Do not let it master you.

I remember shortly after 9/11, it seemed as if the enemy for a brief moment enveloped the entire nation with the fear of flying. As the media kept replaying the horrific images of the planes searing into the twin towers, it seemed as if no one in America would ever dare to fly again.

But glory to God, that evil cloud was soon shattered. It was as if collectively as a people we decided that to desist from flying was to give the terrorist a victory. We defied the fear of terrorism and once again began to fly.

Beloved, in this age of terrorism, as long as God is leading you on your journey, do not be afraid to travel. Board your plane with confidence, get on the subways, drive on the highways, ride on the buses...do not let anything stop you. Do not be afraid.

> Do the things you fear, and the death of fear is certain!

Even in the midst of an unstable world economy, you do not need to be afraid of the future. Your economy is not of the earth. You are positioned in the heavenlies where provision is inexhaustible.

Do not give fear a chance in your life. Take strong action against fear. Anytime it confronts you, chase it out. Declare an all-out war against any form of fear in your life. Determine to *fight to the finish*. Go ahead, dream big. Aim high. Have no fear of failure. You have dominion!

4. OVERCOME FEAR BY BUILDING YOUR FAITH!

The level of victory and dominion that you will enjoy over fear largely depends on your level of faith. Jesus said, "Be it unto you according to your faith." Also Habakkuk 2:4b states, "*...But the just shall live by his faith.*"

The enemy is constantly warring and fighting against you to weaken your faith. If satan can cause your faith to fail, then he knows that he has gotten you where he wants you—in a state of fear and bondage. And fear opens the door for him to wreak all manner of havoc. To prevent this from happening, you must never stop "*building yourselves up on your most holy faith*" (Jude 1:20).

Beloved, do not just have faith. Have *growing* faith. Strong and vibrant faith is the fortress that keeps the devil off your life and territory. In the battle of life, faith is your shield. By it, every fiery dart of the wicked one is quenched (Ephesians 6:16). You cannot afford for one moment to be stagnant in your faith. You must keep on growing. You need faith to win life's battles. You need growing faith to sustain your victory!

Do not be intimidated by fearful situations. Tough times are only "invitations" for you to put your faith to work. Do not pass up such opportunities. Embrace them with all your heart. Do not run away. As you face them, your faith will grow.

As you act upon God's Word in faith, your fear will diminish and ultimately be destroyed. If you study the Bible for hours on end, and confess the Scriptures all day long but you never act upon the Word in obedience,

> Strong and vibrant faith is the fortress that keeps the devil off your life and territory.

you will not increase in faith. This is because God's Word and promises will only come alive in your life after you act upon them.

Sitting idly on your shelf, the Bible is just like any other book. It is only until you read it and begin to act upon its words, that you will experience the power of God. One of my mentors in ministry put it this way, "You must first **believe** the Word, **behave** the Word, and then you will **become** the Word."

David had great faith to fight Goliath because he had acted upon God's Word in times past. His previous "trophies of faith," of how he overcame the bear and the lion, strengthened his faith and reassured him as he faced the dreaded giant in battle.

God has a great *track record*. What God did for you in times past are trophies of faith that will keep your faith going strong. The more you remember His past faithfulness, the more your faith will grow. When you know that what God did yesterday, He can do today, your faith will be strengthened. Remember, He *is the same yester-day, today, and forever* (Hebrews 13:8).

> Faith frees you to walk in dominion!

But you will have no track record if you have never acted upon God's Word. On the contrary, as you act on God's Word, your life will be full of testimonies. And the more you experience God's miracles and power in your life, the stronger your faith will become. The more your faith grows, the greater your ability to overcome fear. You will no longer live in bondage. You will be released to walk in dominion. *Faith frees you to walk in dominion!*

YOUR COMMISSION…

'DOMINION' IS GOD'S DIVINE COMMISSION TO YOU

Then God blessed (__put your name here__) and God said to (__put your name here__), "Be fruitful and multiply; fill the earth and subdue it; have dominion over the fish of the sea, over the birds of the air, and over every living thing that moves on the earth."

GENESIS 1:28

In every area of your life—spiritual, physical, financial, material, emotional, social—the Lord wants you to be fruitful and multiply, to fill the earth with His glory and subdue any obstacle that may want to hinder you. God wants you to have dominion in all things. Therefore, it is time for you to rise up from the valley of mediocrity, defeat, and limitation. Rise up and take charge— start walking in dominion!

....Go FORTH AND DOMINATE!

Friend, you do not have to *walk as a servant* when God has destined you to *walk in dominion!*

Go forth and dominate in every area where you had once known defeat. Declare war against the enemy. Subdue him! Anything that is "stealing from you," "killing you," or "destroying you" must no longer be tolerated.

What are the things that are troubling you? Is it sickness, failure, poverty, barrenness? Well, whatever it is, 'it' has a name. Now is the time to move every hindering mountain that has faced you for so long. Call it by name! Serve "it" a "quit notice." In your dominion authority, say to it, "Your time in my life is up!"

> You do not have to *walk as a servant* when God has destined you to *walk in dominion!*

Refuse and resist any form of evil in your life and the lives of your loved ones. Throw out every bad work of the devil with immediate effect. The "works of the devil" are all the things that cause harm, hurt, destruction, pain, and shame. It is anything that makes life unfulfilling and unpleasant. Anything that steals, kills, or destroys.

The thief comes only in order to steal and kill and destroy. **I came that they may have and enjoy life, and have it in abundance (to the full, till it overflows)**.

JOHN 10:10A (AMP)

God, in the Person of the Lord Jesus, came physically to the earth to eradicate those things that are damaging to your wellbeing. Jesus came to destroy every evil work of the devil in your life.

> For this purpose the Son of God was manifested, that He might destroy the works of the devil.
>
> 1 JOHN 3:8B

God is a loving Father. He does not want anything whatsoever to hurt or destroy you. This is why He has given you dominion in Christ. As you exercise your dominion authority, *"Nothing shall by any means hurt you!"* God is good, and He is good all the time. Far be it from your good God to ever do wickedly!

> Surely God will never do wickedly, nor will the Almighty pervert justice.
>
> JOB 34:12

God will never do wickedly! NEVER! He will never orchestrate anything evil against you. On the contrary, His plans and purposes for you are only good.

> For I know the thoughts that I think toward you, says the LORD, thoughts of peace and not of evil, to give you a future and a hope.
>
> JEREMIAH 29:11

Jesus came so that you may enjoy the "good life." There is no reason why you should go through a "grievous" life. He came that you may have an **abundant** life, not an **agonizing** life. The gospel of our Lord Jesus Christ is the message of Good News, not Bad News. He came to bring you hope. He did not come to add to your despair. While He walked the earth, He went about doing good, not evil.

> How God anointed Jesus of **Nazareth** with the Holy Spirit and with power, who went about doing good and healing all who were oppressed by the devil, for God was with Him.

> ACTS 10: 38

God is still doing good. He has not changed. His plans for you are *good.* His gifts are *good.* His blessings are *good.* They make rich and add no sorrow (*Proverbs 10:22*).

> Jesus came so that you may enjoy the "good life." There is no reason why you should go through a "grievous" life!

Whatever is not good in your life is not of God. And it has got to go. So rise above all the things that have kept you down in times past. Break free from every shackle of mediocrity and misery. Ascend to levels of glory and honor that you had never known before. Press into the high quality of life, which God has ordained for you right from the beginning.

Do not accept the **woes** of life. God has made you a **winner**. Do not let the storms of life subdue you...you are destined to be above **only, never** beneath. You were created for **rulership**, not for ruin. You are made for **mastery**, not for **misery**. You are destined to be **a victor**. You are not a **victim**. God created you **to have** dominion!

In the name of Jesus Christ our Lord, I decree an end to every *roller-coaster* experience. You will no longer be up today, and down tomorrow. From now on, your life will be one of never-ending victory and power. You will never again sit in the low places of the earth; you will never again walk like a servant in the earth, but all the days of your life, you will walk in dominion!

Dominion Decree

I AM A MAN OF DOMINION
I LIVE IN DOMINION,
DOMINION OVER SIN, SICKNESSES,
DISEASES, OPPRESSION, POVERTY,
AND ALL THE WICKEDNESS OF THE DEVIL.
I AM AN OUTSTANDING SUCCESS,
I AM A ROLE MODEL, I AM A PACESETTER;
I AM BORN TO WIN, AND BORN TO REIGN!

(DECREE IT! THIS IS WHO YOU ARE IN JESUS' MIGHTY NAME!)

To order additional copies of

Walking In Dominion

have your credit card ready and call
1 800-917-BOOK (2665)
1-866-370-6352

or e-mail
orders@selahbooks.com
info@dominioninternationalcenter.org

or order online at
www.selahbooks.com
www.dominionlifestyle.org